Pocket

BRISBANE
& THE GOLD COAST

TOP SIGHTS · LOCAL LIFE · MADE EASY

D0529188

In This Book

QuickStart Guide

Your keys to understanding the region – we help you decide what to do and how to do it

Need to Know
Tips for a smooth trip

Neighbourhoods
What's where

Explore Brisbane & the Gold Coast

The best things to see and do, neighbourhood by neighbourhood

Top Sights
Make the most of your visit

Local Life
The insider's region

The Best of Brisbane & the Gold Coast

The highlights in handy lists to help you plan

Best Walks
See the city on foot

Brisbane & the Gold Coast's Best...
The best experiences

Survival Guide

Tips and tricks for a seamless, hassle-free experience

Getting Around
Travel like a local

Essential Information
Including where to stay

Our selection of the region's best places to eat, drink and experience:

◎ **Sights**

✖ **Eating**

🍷 **Drinking**

★ **Entertainment**

🔒 **Shopping**

These symbols give you the vital information for each listing:

📞	Telephone Numbers	👪	Family-Friendly
🕐	Opening Hours	🐾	Pet-Friendly
P	Parking	🚌	Bus
🚭	Nonsmoking	⛴	Ferry
@	Internet Access	M	Metro
📶	Wi-Fi Access	S	Subway
🥗	Vegetarian Selection	🚋	Tram
📖	English-Language Menu	🚆	Train

Find each listing quickly on maps for each neighbourhood:

Bar Hemingway

16 📍 Map p233, B2

Legend has it that Hemi
self, wielding a machine
...rate this timber-pan
...ered bar during
...showpiece is a
...en by Papa ar
...town. Dress
...s.com; Hôtel Rit
...; 🕐6.30pm-2a

QuickStart Guide 7

Explore Brisbane & the Gold Coast 21

Worth a Trip:

The Best of Brisbane & the Gold Coast 125

Brisbane & the Gold Coast's Best Walks

Brisbane & the Gold Coast's Best ...

Survival Guide 147

QuickStart Guide

Welcome to Brisbane & the Gold Coast

No longer satisfied to remain in the shadow of Sydney and Melbourne, Brisbane is subverting stereotypes and surprising the critics. Welcome to Australia's new subtropical 'It kid'. A little way south, the Gold Coast is built for pleasure and remains utterly dedicated to sun, surf and the body beautiful; this strip of coast may be Australia's most iconic holiday destination.

Brisbane city skyline at sunset
F11PHOTO/SHUTTERSTOCK ©

Brisbane & the Gold Coast
Top Sights

City Hall (p24)
Brisbane's 'People's Palace' was built in the 1920s.

Gallery of Modern Art (p44)

Australia's biggest gallery of modern and contemporary art.

Brisbane Powerhouse (p82)

An electrifying hub of culture, creativity and arts-loving crowds.

South Bank Parklands (p46)

Luminous sand, swaying palms and crystalline waters.

Gold Coast Theme Parks (p102)

Thrilling rides, water slides, movie sets and fairground fantasy.

D'Aguilar National Park (p40)

Hike, camp and indulge in nature and wildlife.

Brisbane & the Gold Coast Local Life

Local experiences and hidden gems to help you uncover the real region

Get under the skin of Brisbane and the Gold Coast by hanging out in local neighbourhoods, exploring the cafe and bar scenes, scouring weekend markets and surfing some of the lesser-known breaks.

PHILIP QUIRK/GETTY IMAGES ©

West End Walking (p48)
☑ Artisanal coffee and beer
☑ Street art

A Day in Fortitude Valley (p66)
☑ Intriguing shops and galleries
☑ Poolside downtime

New Farm Walk (p84)

☑ Riverside walking ☑ Weekend markets and music

Other great places to experience the region like a local:

An Evening in Coolangatta (p122)

☑ Indie-atmosphere bars ☑ Local pub and surf club

Brisbane & the Gold Coast Day Planner

Day One

Start the day on the indie streets of West End. Charge up with a bottle of cold drip at **Blackstar Coffee Roasters** (p49), bag obscure vinyl at **Jet Black Cat Music** (p49) and pick up a local novel at **Avid Reader** (p63). Wander down West End's sleepier side streets (especially those south of Vulture St) for rustic, peeling Queenslanders (traditional Queensland houses) or head straight up Boundary St to the street-art murals of the **Pillars Project** (p52).

Spend the afternoon exploring Brisbane's riverside South Bank precinct. Make time for the outstanding **Gallery of Modern Art** (p44) or pop into the **Queensland Art Gallery** (p53) for more traditional masterpieces. Both galleries harbour alfresco cafes for a mid-afternoon pit stop. Continue along the river to **South Bank Parklands** (p46), home to a Nepalese Peace Pagoda.

After dinner, catch a ferry for glittering views of the city skyline. Alight at Eagle St Pier, from where the booze and blues of the **Brooklyn Standard** (p34) is a short walk away. Even closer is **Mr & Mrs G Riverbar** (p36), perfect for a waterfront nightcap.

Day Two

Start day two in Brisbane's lively city centre, taking time to soak up its eclectic mix of old and new architecture. Top billing goes to Brisbane's impressive **City Hall** (p24), which offers fascinating guided tours of its architectural marvels and soaring clock tower. Make time for the building's highly engaging **Museum of Brisbane** (p25).

Post-lunch, head south along George St, a street dotted with beautiful examples of heritage architecture, among them Treasury Building, the Mansions and **Parliament House** (p28). Detour to **Coffee Anthology** (p34) or **John Mills Himself** (p35) along the way before ambling through the verdant beauty of the **City Botanic Gardens** (p28).

Bar Alto is located in a power station that has been converted into a buzzing culture hub, **Brisbane Powerhouse** (p82), making it a handy dining option if you've booked to see a show. In the summer months, it's equally convenient if you're planning on catching a flick at **Moonlight Cinema** (p92), set up right next door in New Farm Park. If not, head to Newstead for a rocking epilogue at live-music 'It kid' the **Triffid** (p91).

Short on time?
We've arranged Brisbane & the Gold Coast's must-sees into these day-by-day itineraries to make sure you see the very best of the region in the time you have available.

Day Three

☀ Start the day with a thrill at **Riverlife** (p97), where you can hire kayaks and bikes for some riverside action, or book a rock-climbing adventure up the vertiginous Kangaroo Point Cliffs. For something more sedate, head to nearby Woolloongabba and lose yourself inside retro nirvana **Woolloongabba Antique Centre** (p101). Done, then zip across town to Fortitude Valley.

☀ Explore the Valley. Shop for local jewellery at **Miss Bond** (p67), rare fragrances at **Libertine** (p67) or old-school Aussie rock at **Butter Beats** (p79). Call in at high-end **Fallow** (p78) for avant-garde pieces Kanye would approve of. For a culture fix, check out **Institute of Modern Art** (p69) or pocket rocket **TW Fine Art** (p67). Then style up and head up to rooftop **Eleven** (p73) for a sunset martini.

☾ Depending on what time you dine, your evening Valley options are varied and eclectic. You might catch a contemporary dance performance at the **Judith Wright Centre of Contemporary Arts** (p77), A-list DJs at **Family** (p74), a drag show at **Beat MegaClub** (p77) or an art-house film at **Palace Centro** (p77). *Don't wait up!*

Day Four

☀ It's time to hit the Gold Coast beaches. Start early (in summer the sun is up at 4.30am) with a walk, swim or surf at any of the main beach strips, such as Surfers Paradise, Main Beach or Broadbeach. Head in for a healthy breakfast and strong coffee at **Bumbles Cafe** (p110) or **Providore** (p109). Scale the tallest tower to **SkyPoint Observation Deck** (p108) for sweeping coast and hinterland views before lunch at **Marina Mirage** (p111) by the Broadwater.

☀ Then it's time for a stand-up paddleboard lesson, or a visit to the native animals at **Currumbin Wildlife Sanctuary** (p116) or **David Fleay Wildlife Park** (p116).

☾ Beachside sundowner beers at the **Coolangatta Hotel** (p123) await or head to one of Burleigh's excellent breweries or the surf club. Dinner at **Rick Shores** (p118) and a nightcap at **Justin Lane** (p119) rooftop.

Need to Know

**For more information,
see Survival Guide (p147)**

Currency
Australian dollar ($)

Language
English

Visas
All visitors to Australia need a visa, except New Zealanders. Apply online for an ETA or eVisitor visa, each allowing a three-month stay: www.border.gov.au.

Money
ATMs are widely available in Brisbane. Credit cards are accepted in most hotels, restaurants and cafes.

Mobile Phones
Australia's mobile networks are GSM networks with 4G service, so most visitors can use an Australian SIM card in their exisiting phone. This usually works out cheaper than using your home SIM and incurring expensive roaming charges.

Time
Australian Eastern Standard Time (GMT/UCT plus 10 hours). Daylight saving time is not observed in Queensland.

Tipping
Tipping isn't traditionally part of Australian etiquette, but it's increasingly the norm to tip around 10% for good service in restaurants, and a few dollars for porters (bellhops) and taxi rides.

① Before You Go

Your Daily Budget

Budget: Less than $150
▶ Dorm bed: $25–38 per night
▶ Burger or cheap Asian meal: $10–20
▶ City to West End bus ride: $5.60

Midrange: $150–300
▶ Double room in a midrange hotel: $120–200
▶ Breakfast or lunch in a cafe: $20–40
▶ Ticketed exhibition at GOMA: $18–25

Top End: More than $300
▶ Double room in a top-end hotel: from $210
▶ Dinner at a top-tier restaurant: from $90
▶ Opera or theatre show: $65–185

Useful Websites

Lonely Planet (www.lonelyplanet.com/australia/queensland/brisbane) Destination information, hotel bookings, traveller forum and more.

Visit Brisbane (www.visitbrisbane.com.au) Brisbane's official tourism website.

Broadsheet Brisbane (www.broadsheet.com.au/brisbane) Reviews of the city's hot spots.

Four Thousand (www.fourthousand.com.au) Weekly round-up of (cool) local goings on.

Advance Planning

Three months before Book accommodation, especially if visiting during busy festival or holiday periods.

One month before Reserve tickets to major performing arts and sporting events.

Two weeks before Reserve a table at a top restaurant.

② Arriving in Brisbane & the Gold Coast

From Brisbane Airport

Brisbane Airport (www.bne.com.au; Airport Dr) is the main international gateway to the greater Brisbane region, with frequent and extensive domestic connections, as well as nonstop international flights to New Zealand, the Pacific islands, North America and Asia.

Frequent Airtrain (☑1800 119 091; www.airtrain.com.au; adult one way/return $17.50/33) services connect Brisbane Airport's two terminals to central Brisbane. Stops include Roma St Station, adjacent to Brisbane's main long-distance bus terminal.

Con-X-ion (☑1300 370 471; www.con-x-ion.com) runs regular shuttle buses between the airport and hotels in the Brisbane city centre (one way/return $20/36). It also connects Brisbane Airport to Gold Coast hotels and private residences (one way/return $49/92).

From Gold Coast Airport

Gold Coast Airport (www.goldcoastairport.com.au; Longa Ave, Bilinga) is in Coolangatta, 25km south of Surfers Paradise.

Gold Coast Tourist Shuttle (☑07-5574 5111, 1300 655 655; www.gcshuttle.com.au; one way adult/child $22/13) Meets flights into Gold Coast Airport and transfers to most Gold Coast accommodation. Also runs to Gold Coast theme parks.

Con-X-ion Airport Transfers (☑1300 266 946; www.con-x-ion.com) Runs transfers to/from Gold Coast Airport (one way adult/child from $22/13), Brisbane airport (one way from adult/child $49/25) and Gold Coast theme parks.

③ Getting Around

🚢 Boat

CityCat (☑13 12 30; www.translink.com.au; one way $5.60; ⏱5.25am-11.25pm) catamarans service 18 ferry terminals between St Lucia and Northshore Hamilton. Free CityHopper ferries zigzag back and forth across the water between North Quay, South Bank, the CBD, Kangaroo Point and Sydney St in New Farm.

Cross River Ferries connect Kangaroo Point with the CBD, and New Farm Park with Norman Park on the adjacent shore.

🚌 Bus

In the city centre, the main stops for local buses are the underground Queen Street Bus Station and King George Square Bus Station.

▸ CityGlider and BUZ services are high-frequency services along busy routes. Tickets cannot be purchased on-board CityGlider and BUZ services; use a **Go Card** (www.translink.com.au/tickets-and-fares/go-card; starting balance adult/child $10/5).

▸ Free, hop-on, hop-off City Loop and Spring Hill Loop bus services circle the CBD and Spring Hill, stopping at key spots including QUT, Queen Street Mall, City Botanic Gardens, Central Station and Roma Street Parkland.

🚕 Taxi

The main taxi companies are **Black & White** (☑13 32 22; www.blackandwhitecabs.com.au) and **Yellow Cab Co** (☑13 19 24; www.yellowcab.com.au). NightLink flat-fare taxis run on Friday and Saturday nights.

🚃 Train

TransLink's **Citytrain network** (www.translink.com.au) has six main lines. All trains go through Roma St Station, Central Station and Fortitude Valley Station. The **Airtrain** (☑1800 119 091; www.airtrain.com.au; adult one way/return $17.50/33) service integrates with the Citytrain network.

Brisbane
Neighbourhoods

Fortitude Valley (p64)
Fortitude Valley is packed with thumping dance clubs, pubs and rocking music venues. Add to this a slew of art galleries and the heady scents of Chinatown and you have one of Brisbane's most intriguing corners.

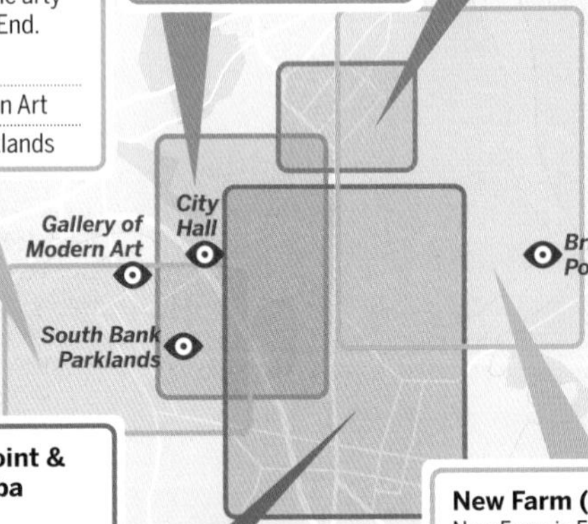

Central Brisbane (p22)
Past, present and future collide in Brisbane's compact heart, an architectural jumble where glittering skyscrapers look down on heritage beauties.
Top Sight
City Hall

South Bank (p42)
Cross-river South Bank dedicates itself to the finer things in life: cultural institutions, the green South Bank Parklands and the arty enclave of West End.
Top Sights
Gallery of Modern Art
South Bank Parklands

Gallery of Modern Art
City Hall
South Bank Parklands
Brisbane Powerhouse

Kangaroo Point & Woollongabba (p94)
Kangaroo Point's imposing Story Bridge and vertiginous western cliffs offer blockbuster views of the Brisbane skyline, while Woolloongabba has heritage facades, antique stores and atmospheric eateries.

New Farm (p80)
New Farm is Fortitude Valley's comfortable neighbour, a verdant corner of graceful Queenslander homes, moderne apartment blocks and lush subtropical gardens.
Top Sight
Brisbane Powerhouse

The Gold Coast
Neighbourhoods

Worth a Trip

⊙ **Top Sights**

D'Aguilar National Park (p40)

Theme Parks (p102)

Surfers Paradise & Main Beach (p104)
Beach, fun and sun with something for everyone! Surfers Paradise's malls and mega-clubs let the party-hard kids have their fun, while other neighbourhoods such as Main Beach and Broadbeach corner coastal chic.

Burleigh Heads & Currumbin (p112)
Burleigh Heads has a retro charm and booming culinary scene. That famous right-hand point break still pumps while the beautiful pine-backed beach continues to charm everyone who lays eyes on it.

Worth a Trip

○ **Local Life**

Coolangatta (p122)

Explore
Brisbane & the Gold Coast

Worth a Trip

Post Office Sq (p126)
YMGERMAN/GETTY IMAGES ©

Explore

Central Brisbane

Historic buildings form the bulk of central Brisbane's sights, especially on or around George St. The Roma Street Parklands and City Botanic Gardens form the city centre's northern and southern bookends, while its eastern edge is lined with a lively riverside promenade. Central Brisbane is best explored on foot.

The Sights in a Day

☀ Grab a morning takeaway from **Coffee Anthology** (p34) and saunter through the nearby **City Botanic Gardens** (p28; pictured left) before the heat sets in. Catch an exhibition at the nearby **QUT Art Museum** (p30) on George St, a street worth strolling down for its cachet of beautiful heritage buildings, among them Parliament House, the Mansions and Treasury.

☀ After lunch, head to King George Sq and Brisbane's monumental **City Hall** (p24). Consider joining a tour of the building or, at the very least, spend an hour or so exploring its innovative **Museum of Brisbane** (p25), which offers a fresh perspective on the city's past and present. From here, head east along Adelaide St and turn right into Edward St, the city's blue-ribbon retail strip.

☾ On the corner of Edward and Mary Sts is **Folio Books** (p39), one of the city's best bookshops and a good place to pick up some local fiction or a coffee-table tome on Queensland history or architecture. One block east, Mary St becomes Eagle St, the latter offering an impressive view of Brisbane's skyscrapers. Close by is Eagle St Pier and its waterfront promenade. Wrap things up with a cooling toast at **Mr & Mrs G Riverbar** (p36).

◉ Top Sights

City Hall (p24)

♥ Best of Brisbane & the Gold Coast

Eating

Miel Container (p31)

Felix For Goodness (p31)

Urbane (p33)

Cha Cha Char (p33)

Drinking

Gresham Bar (p34)

Mr & Mrs G Riverbar (p36)

Brooklyn Standard (p34)

Shopping

Noosa Chocolate Factory (p38)

Maiocchi (p38)

Jan Powers Farmers Market (p31)

Getting There

🚆 **Train** All six metropolitan lines run through Central Station and Roma St Station.

🚌 **Bus** Most metropolitan bus routes run through the city centre. The main stops are the underground Queen St Bus Station and King George Sq Bus Station. Free, weekday City Loop and Spring Hill Loop bus services circle the CBD and Spring Hill.

Top Sights
City Hall

City Hall is Brisbane's heritage headliner, a sandstone Alpha commanding King George Square. Costing A£1 million, the building became Australia's most expensive civic space when completed in 1930. It remains one of its grandest public buildings, fronted by a row of sequoia-sized Corinthian columns, clad in luminous Helidon sandstone and heaving with beautiful craftsmanship, historical anecdotes and cultural treasures.

Map p26, B4

07-3339 0845

www.brisbane.qld.gov.au

King George Sq

admission free

8am-5pm Mon-Fri, 9am-5pm Sat & Sun

Central

City Hall Auditorium

Auditorium

City Hall's most impressive feature, however, is its auditorium. A magnificent, circular space inspired by Rome's ancient Pantheon, its highlights include precious mahogany and blue-gum floors, a restored 4300-pipe organ by Henry Willis & Sons, as well as a plaster frieze by local artist Daphne Mayo. Above it all is the dashing dome, kitted out in thousands of LED lights which, when switched on, produce a spectacular light show. The Rolling Stones played their first-ever Australian gig in the auditorium in 1965, and the space now hosts free music concerts every Tuesday at noon.

Museum of Brisbane

Located on City Hall's 3rd floor, the wonderfully interactive **Museum of Brisbane** (07-3339 0800; www.museumofbrisbane.com.au; Level 3, Brisbane City Hall, King George Sq; admission free; 10am-5pm; Central) offers a fresh take on the city's past and present. The current hero exhibition is 100% Brisbane. An innovative collaboration between the museum and Berlin-based theatre company Rimini Protokoll, the project sheds light on the lives of 100 current Brisbane residents, who together accurately reflect the city's population based on data from the Australian Bureau of Statistics (ABS). The result is a snapshot of a metropolis much more complex than you may have expected.

Clocktower

Modelled on St Mark's bell tower in Venice, the tower's four clock faces are among the largest in the country. The clock consists of Westminster chimes, ringing every 15 minutes on weekdays. For a commanding view of central Brisbane, head on up to the tower's observation platform, perched a lofty 76m above street level. The platform is reached via a charming vintage lift, one of the oldest still in operation in Australia.

☑ Top Tips

▶ Tickets to the clock tower are free and allocated on a first-come, first-served basis. Grab your tickets at the Museum of Brisbane reception counter and consider heading in early during holiday periods as allocations can fill up quickly during busy times.

▶ For a more comprehensive exploration of City Hall's architectural treasures, opt for the free, 45-minute guided tour of the building, which also includes access to the clock tower. Although tickets should be booked in advance by phone, they're often available on the day from the Museum of Brisbane, so always ask if space is available.

✗ Take a Break

City Hall is located close to a number of great eating options, including newcomer Greenglass (p32), a loft-style space with French-inspired dishes and gorgeous wines by the glass.

For reviews see

◉	Top Sights	p24
◉	Sights	p28
⊗	Eating	p31
◔	Drinking	p34
⊕	Entertainment	p36
⊜	Shopping	p38

Sights

City Botanic Gardens PARK

1 ◎ Map p26, D7

Originally a collection of food crops planted by convicts in 1825, this is Brisbane's favourite green space. Descending gently from the Queensland University of Technology campus to the river, its mass of lawns, tangled Moreton Bay figs, bunya pines, macadamia trees and tai chi troupes are a soothing elixir for frazzled urbanites. Free, one-hour guided tours leave the rotunda at 11am and 1pm daily, and the gardens host the popular Brisbane Riverside Markets (p31) on Sunday. Ditch the gardens' average cafe for a picnic. (www.brisbane.qld.gov.au; Alice St; admission free; ⊙24hr; ☺QUT Gardens Point, ☒Central)

Local Life
Free BBQs

Locals love a 'barbie' and you'll find no shortage of people making good use of the free electric barbecues dotted throughout the beautiful **Roma Street Parkland** (Map p26, A2; www.visitbrisbane.com.au/Roma-Street-Parkland-and-Spring-Hill; 1 Parkland Blvd; admission free; ⊙24hr; ☒Roma St). Pack some local produce and beers, head in early to secure a spot by the coveted lakeside, and bask in the 'Aussie dream'.

Parliament House HISTORIC BUILDING

2 ◎ Map p26, C7

With a roof clad in Mt Isa copper, this lovely blanched-white stone, French Renaissance–style building dates from 1868 and overlooks the City Botanic Gardens. The only way to peek inside is on one of the free tours, which leave on demand at the listed times (2pm only when parliament is sitting). Arrive five minutes before tours begin; no need to book. (www.parliament.qld.gov. au; cnr Alice & George Sts; admission free; ⊙tours 1pm, 2pm, 3pm & 4pm nonsitting days; ☺QUT Gardens Point, ☒Central)

Old Government House HISTORIC BUILDING

3 ◎ Map p26, D7

Hailed as Queensland's most important historic building, this 1862 showpiece was designed by estimable government architect Charles Tiffin as a plush residence for Sir George Bowen, Queensland's first governor. The lavish innards were restored in 2009 and the property now offers free podcast and guided tours; the latter must be booked by phone or email. The building also houses the William Robinson Gallery, dedicated to the Australian artist and home to an impressive collection of his works, including two Archibald Prize–winning paintings. (☏07-3138 8005; www.ogh.qut. edu.au; 2 George St; admission free; ⊙9am-4pm, 1hr guided tours 10.30am Tue-Thu; ☺QUT Gardens Point, ☒Central)

RICHARD I'ANSON/GETTY IMAGES ©

Parliament House

St John's Cathedral
CHURCH

4 ⊙ Map p26, D2

A magnificent fusion of stone, carved timber and stained glass just west of Fortitude Valley, St John's Cathedral is a beautiful example of 19th-century Gothic Revival architecture. The building is a true labour of love: construction began in 1906 and wasn't finished until 2009, making it one of the world's last cathedrals of this architectural style to be completed. (☎07-3835 2222; www.stjohnscathedral.com.au; 373 Ann St; ⏱9.30am-4.30pm; ▯Central)

Commissariat Store Museum
MUSEUM

5 ⊙ Map p26, B6

Built by convicts in 1829, this former government storehouse is the oldest occupied building in Brisbane. Inside is an immaculate little museum devoted to convict and colonial history. Don't miss the convict 'fingers' and the exhibit on Italians in Queensland. (www.queenslandhistory.org; 115 William St; adult/child/family $6/3/12; ⏱10am-4pm Tue-Fri; ☒North Quay, ▯Central)

Top Tip

CityHopper

Getting around Brisbane can be half the fun if you use river transport. The CityHopper, a half-hourly, free, inner-city ferry service, is a gorgeous way to hop between South Bank, the CBD (Central Business District) and leafy New Farm. Buy a Go Card, allowing you to travel on all TransLink city buses, ferries and rail services, as well as on TransLink trains, buses and light rail on the Gold Coast. Fares work out at least 30% cheaper than if using single paper tickets.

QUT Art Museum

MUSEUM

 6   Map p26, C7

Head to this little champ for regularly changing exhibits of contemporary Australian art and works by Brisbane art students, plus temporary exhibits, some by prolific international artists. The museum is located on campus at the Queensland University of Technology. (07-3138 5370; www.artmuseum.qut.edu.au; 2 George St; admission free; 10am-5pm Tue-Fri, noon-4pm Sat & Sun; QUT Gardens Point, Central)

Brisbane Greeters

TOURS

7   Map p26, B4

Free, small-group, hand-held introductory tours of Brizzy with affable volunteers. Book at least three days in advance, either online or by phone. Booking online allows you to opt for a 'Your Choice' tour, based on your personal interests and schedule. Note that 'Your Choice' tours should be booked at least five days in advance. (07-3156 6364; www.brisbanegreeters.com.au; Brisbane City Hall, King George Sq; 10am)

Spring Hill Baths

SWIMMING

8   Map p26, A1

Opened in 1886, this quaint heated 25m pool was the city's first in-ground pool. Still encircled by its cute timber change rooms, it's one of the oldest public baths in the southern hemisphere. (1300 332 583; www.cityaquaticsandhealth.com.au; 14 Torrington St, Spring Hill; adult/child/family $5.40/3.90/16.40; 6.30am-7pm Mon-Thu, to 6pm Fri, 8am-5pm Sat, 8am-1pm Sun; 30, 321)

Brisbane Explorer

TOURS

9   Map p26, C3

This hop-on, hop-off shuttle bus wheels past 15 Brisbane landmarks (in 1½ hours if you don't jump off), including the CBD, Mt Coot-tha, Chinatown, South Bank and Story Bridge. Tours depart every 45 minutes from Post Office Sq on Queen St. Buy tickets online or from the driver. A second, five-stop tour is also offered, taking in the Brisbane Botanic Gardens and Mt Coot-tha. (02-9567 8400; www.brisbanecityexplorer.com.au; day tickets adult/child/family $40/25/110; 9am-5.15pm)

Eating

Miel Container

BURGERS $

10 🍴 Map p26, C5

Planted in a nook below Brisbane's skyscrapers, this rude-red shipping container flips outstanding burgers. Choose your bun, your burger, your veggies, cheese and sauces, then search for a spare seat by the footpath. If it's all too hard, opt for the classic Miel grass-fed-beef burger with onion jam, bacon and bush tomato. Succulent, meaty bliss. (📞07-3229 4883; www.facebook.com/mielcontainer; cnr Mary & Albert Sts; burgers from $12; ⏲11am-10pm Mon-Thu & Sat, to 11pm Fri; 🚉Central)

Felix for Goodness

CAFE $

11 🍴 Map p26, B4

Felix channels Melbourne with its arty laneway locale, industrial fit-out and effortlessly cool vibe. Sip espresso or chow down decent brunch grub such as spelt poppy-seed pikelets with vanilla cream, saffron cardamom and poached pears, or pumpkin, ricotta and caramelised onion frittata. A short evening menu focuses on bar bites (best paired with a creative cocktail), with the odd pasta or risotto main. (📞07-3161 7966; www.felixforgoodness.com; 50 Burnett Lane; mains lunch $12-22, dinner $23-24; ⏲7am-2.30pm Mon & Tue, to 9.30pm Wed-Fri, 8am-2pm Sat; 🚉🖊; 🚉Central)

Strauss

CAFE $

12 🍴 Map p26, C4

Strauss bucks its corporate surrounds with low-key cool and a neighbourly vibe. Head in for pastries or a short, competent, locavore menu of creative salads, thick-cut toasted sandwiches (go for the pastrami, sauerkraut, cheese and pickle combo) and upgraded classics such as French toast paired with lemon curd and labne. The place takes its coffee seriously, with cold brew and rotating espresso and filtered options. (📞07-3236 5232; www.straussfd.com; 189 Elizabeth St; dishes $6.50-13.50; ⏲6.30am-3pm Mon-Fri; 🛜; 🚉Central)

Q Local Life

Markets

On Wednesday, Reddacliff Pl (outside Treasury) transforms into the **Jan Powers Farmers Market** (Map p26, B5; www.janpowersfarmersmarkets.com.au; Reddacliff Pl, George St; ⏲8am-6pm Wed; 🚌North Quay, 🚉Central), with local growers and producers selling an appetite-piquing selection of produce and artisan edibles. On Sunday, locals graze, browse and groove to live bands at the **Brisbane Riverside Markets** (Map p26, D6; 📞07-3870 2807; www.facebook.com/brisbaneriversidemarkets; City Botanic Gardens, Alice St; ⏲8am-3pm Sun; 🚌QUT Gardens Point, 🚉Central).

AJ Vietnamese Noodle House

VIETNAMESE $

 13 Map p26, C5

When it all gets too much, find solace in a steaming bowl of *pho* (Vietnamese noodle soup) at this cheap, humble bolt-hole. AJ's broth is fragrant and delicate, and there's a number of variations, including spicy beef noodle soup and a BBQ-pork wonton noodle with veggies. If you're especially hungry, devour a side of rice-paper rolls. (07-3229 2128; www.aj-vietnamese-noodle-house.com.au; 70 Charlotte St; mains $11-15; 11.30am-3pm & 5-9pm Mon-Fri, 11.30am-9pm Sat; Central)

Greenglass

FRENCH $$

14 Map p26, A4

Up a flight of stairs wedged between a discount chemist and a topless bar is this pared-back, loft-style newcomer. Head up for novel breakfast items such as a charcoal bun filled with fried egg, avocado and thinly sliced pork belly, French-centric bistro lunch dishes and an enlightened wine list that favours small-batch Australian drops. (www.facebook.com/greenglass336; 336 George St; lunch $12-30, dinner mains $18-35; 7am-9pm Mon-Fri; Roma St)

St John's Cathedral (p29)

Hanaichi   JAPANESE $$

15 Map p26, C4

Ride the sushi train out of Hunger Central at Hanaichi, where the revolving track packs in the lunchtime passengers. Also on offer are bento boxes, soups and an à la carte menu, if you'd rather take your time. Japanese beers, sake, plum wine and vodka available too. (☑07-3210 0032; www.hanaichisushi bar.com.au; Level 1, Wintergarden Centre, 171 Queen St; sushi $3.50-8, mains $14-25; ⏱11.30am-9pm Sun-Thu, to 10pm Fri & Sat; 🚉Central)

Urbane   MODERN AUSTRALIAN $$$

16 Map p26, D5

Argentinian chef Alejandro Cancino heads intimate Urbane, the apotheosis of Brisbane fine dining. If the budget permits, opt for the eight-course degustation, which does more justice to Cancino's talents. Needless to say, dishes intrigue and delight, whether it's corn 'snow' (made by dropping corn mousse into liquid nitrogen) or pickled onion petals filled with tapioca pearls and regional macadamia nuts. The wine list is smashing. (☑07-3229 2271; www.urbanerestaurant.com; 181 Mary St; 5-course menu $110, 7-course menu $145; ⏱6-10.30pm Tue-Sat; 🍴; 🚢Eagle St Pier, 🚉Central)

Cha Cha Char   STEAK $$$

17 Map p26, D4

Fastidious carnivores drool at the mere mention of this linen-tabled

 Top Tip

Set Lunch

A number of top-tier city restaurants – including Esquire – offer set lunch degustation menus that cost significantly less than their dinner menus. Some are offered throughout the working week, others only on a set day. Check individual restaurant websites for details and always book in advance.

steakhouse, famed for its wood-fired slabs of premium Australian beef. Rib, rump and T-bone aside, the kitchen also offers first-rate seafood and roast game dishes including paperbark-smoked duck breast with roasted mushrooms, pomme fondant, grilled baby zucchinis and pomegranate jus. Part of the Eagle St Pier complex, the dining room's floor-to-ceiling windows come with river views. (☑07-3211 9944; www.chachachar.com.au; 5/1 Eagle St Pier; mains $35-90; ⏱noon-11pm Mon-Fri, 6-11pm Sat & Sun; 🚢Eagle St Pier, 🚉Central)

Esquire   MODERN AUSTRALIAN $$$

18 Map p26, D3

At its best, stark, modernist Esquire transforms top-tier Australian produce into out-of-the-box revelations. While not all creations hit the mark, many do, and you'll get the best value for money by opting for the cheaper set lunch menu. Expect the unexpected, whether it's a smashing fermented lettuce with crunchy garlic and gastrique, or a subversive epilogue of porcini butter cake with hay cream. Book ahead. (☎07-3220 2123; www.esquire.net.au; 145 Eagle St; set menu lunch $60-85, dinner $110-150; ⏰noon-2pm & 6-9pm Tue-Fri, 6-9pm Sat; ⛴Riverside, ⓡCentral)

Drinking

Super Whatnot BAR

19 🍸 Map p26, B4

Trailblazing Super Whatnot remains one of Brisbane's coolest drinking holes, an industrial, split-level playpen in a former beauty school. Slip inside for cognoscenti craft beers, decent vino and crafty cocktails, served to a pleasure-seeking mix of indie kids and thirsty suits. Bar bites include cheeky hot dogs and nachos. (☎07-3210 2343; www.superwhatnot.com; 48 Burnett Lane; ⏰3-11pm Mon-Thu, noon-1am Fri, 3pm-1am Sat, 3-8pm Sun; ⓡCentral)

Brooklyn Standard BAR

20 🍸 Map p26, D3

The red neon sign sets the tone: 'If the music is too loud, you are too old'. And loud, live, nightly tunes are what you get in this rocking cellar bar, decked out in NYC paraphernalia and buzzing with a mixed-age crowd. Stay authentic with a Brooklyn lager or knock back a kooky cocktail (either way, the pretzels are on the house). (☎0405 414 131; www.facebook.com/brooklynstandardbar; Eagle Lane; ⏰4pm-late Mon-Fri, 6pm-late Sat; ⛴Riverside, ⓡCentral)

Coffee Anthology CAFE

21 🍸 Map p26, C6

True to its name, Coffee Anthology keeps caffeine geeks hyped with a rotating selection of specialist blends from cult-status roasters including Padre and Industry Beans. Tasting notes guide the indecisive, and you can even buy a bag or two if you like what's in your cup. Friendly, breezy and contemporary, the place also serves simple breakfast and lunch bites, from porridge and muffins to bagels. (☎07-3210 1881; www.facebook.com/coffeeanthology; 126 Margaret St; ⏰7am-3.30pm Mon-Fri, to noon Sat; 🛜; ⓡCentral)

Nant BAR

22 🍸 Map p26, D5

Leather couches, high ceilings and affable bar staff underscore this moody speakeasy, a showcase for Nant whisky – a superb, internationally renowned single malt from Tasmania's central highlands. Other on-shelf wonders include cognoscenti bourbons, ryes and Prohibition-style gins; taste a few too many, then wobble into the City Botanic Gardens to look for bats. (☎07-3180 2769; www.nant.com.au; 2 Edward St; ⏰noon-late Tue-Sat; ⛴Eagle St Pier, ⓡCentral)

Gresham Bar BAR

23 🍸 Map p26, C3

Tucked into one corner of a noble, heritage-listed bank building, the Gresham evokes the old-school bars of

New York; we're talking pressed-metal ceiling, Chesterfields and a glowing cascade of spirit bottles behind a handsome timber bar (complete with library-style ladder). It's a dark, buzzing, convivial spot, with an especially robust selection of whiskies and a snug side room you'll find difficult to leave. (www.thegresham.com.au; 308 Queen St; ☉7am-3am Mon-Fri, 4pm-3am Sat & Sun; 🛜; 🚉Central)

John Mills Himself
CAFE, BAR

24 Map p26, C5

No doubt Mr Mills would approve of this secret little coffee shop, occupying the very building in which he ran a printing business last century. Accessible from both Charlotte St and an alley off Elizabeth St, its marble bar and penny-tile floors set a very Brooklyn scene for top third-wave coffee. Later in the day, cafe becomes intimate bar, pouring craft Australian beers and spirits. (📞bar 0421 959 865, cafe 0434 064 349; www.johnmillshimself.com.au; 40 Charlotte St; ☉cafe 6.30am-3.30pm Mon-Fri, bar 4-10pm Tue-Thu, to midnight Fri; 🚉Central)

Coppa Spuntino
WINE BAR

25 Map p26, C3

Wrap up the day the Italian way at Coppa Spuntino, a slinky, contemporary wine bar with cut-price house vino, Peroni and Aperol spritz from 4.30pm to 6.30pm. Speckled with architect lamps, it's a grown-up spot for a swill and a nibble (*spuntino* means

---

Understand
Brisbane Floods

Imagine the shocked faces in 2011 when Aussies flicked on the nightly news and saw swirls of brown river water flowing through downtown Brisbane! Wild weather across the Sunshine State caused major inundations, with Australia's third-largest city recording its biggest flood since 1974. Boats, pontoons, ferry docks, the city's excellent Riverwalk walkway network and even a riverside restaurant were all picked up and carried off downstream. More than 30,000 homes in low-lying suburbs were swamped. The clean-up was quick, but then in 2013 it happened again – not as severe this time, but still devastating for locals who had just finished scraping the river mud out of their houses from 2011.

In 2014 a class action was launched by more than 4000 flood victims, alleging the mismanagement of the upstream Wivenhoe and Somerset dams during the 2011 floods. Oddly, the Queensland court regime doesn't support class actions, so the case was actually lodged in the Supreme Court of New South Wales.

The Brisbane River: defining and defiling the city all at once.

snack in Italian), with share-friendly bites including cheese, charcuterie and wood-fired pizzas. A mostly Italian wine list includes natural drops. (📞07-3221 3548; www.coppaspuntino.com; 4/88 Creek St; ⏰7am-9pm Mon-Wed, to 10pm Thu, to 11pm Fri; 🚊Central)

Mr & Mrs G Riverbar   BAR

26 📍 Map p26, D4

Mr & Mrs G spoils guests with curving floor-to-ceiling windows overlooking the river, skyline and Story Bridge. It's a casually chic affair, with vibrantly coloured bar stools, cushy slipper chairs and hand-painted Moroccan side tables on which to rest your glass of chenin blanc. If you're feeling peckish, generous tapas dishes include succulent *keftethes* (Greek-style meatballs), cheese and charcuterie. (📞07-3221 7001; www.mrandmrsg.com. au; Eagle St Pier, 1 Eagle St; ⏰3-10pm Mon & Tue, noon-11pm Wed & Thu, noon-midnight Fri & Sat, noon-10pm Sun; 🛥Eagle St Pier, 🚊Central)

Lefty's Old
Time Music Hall   BAR

27 📍 Map p26, A3

Paint the town and the front porch too, there's a honky-tonk bar in Brisvegas! Tarted up in chandeliers and mounted moose heads (yep, those are bras hanging off the antlers), scarlet-hued Lefty's keeps the good times rolling with close to 200 whiskies and the sweet twang of live country and western. A short, star-spangled food menu includes chilli cheese fries and southern fried chicken. (www.leftysold timemusichall.com; 15 Caxton St, Petrie Tce; ⏰5pm-late Tue-Sun; 🚌375)

Sazerac Bar   BAR

28 📍 Map p26, C5

While the space itself is a little peculiar (the gym flooring reveals its previous life), the floor-to-ceiling view is undisputedly shashing. Perched atop the Four Points by Sheraton (www.fourpointsbrisbane.com) hotel, this is Brisbane's highest bar, with a skyline panorama any CEO would steal for. (📞07-3164 4000; www.sazerac barbrisbane.com; Four Points by Sheraton, Level 30, 99 Mary St; ⏰3-11pm Mon-Thu, from noon Fri-Sun; 🚊Central)

Entertainment

Underground Opera   OPERA

29 ⭐ Map p26, B3

A professional, Brisbane-based performing-arts company running annual seasons of opera and Broadway musical recitals in the subterranean Spring Hill Reservoir, built between 1871 and 1882. See the website for season dates and prices. (📞07-3389 0135, 0429 536 472; www.undergroundopera. com.au; Spring Hill Reservoir, Wickham Tce, Spring Hill; ⏰hours vary; 🚌30, 🚊Central)

Archives Fine Books (p38)

Riverstage

LIVE MUSIC

30 ⭐ Map p26, D8

Evocatively set in the Botanic Gardens, this outdoor arena hosts no shortage of prolific national and international music acts. Past performers include U2, 5 Seconds of Summer, Ellie Goulding and Flume. (☏07-3403 7921; www.brisbane.qld.gov.au/facilities-recreation/arts-and-culture/riverstage; 59 Gardens Point Rd; 🚢QUT Gardens Point, 🚉Central)

Metro Arts Centre

ARTS CENTRE

31 ⭐ Map p26, D5

This downtown venue hosts community theatre, local dramatic pieces, dance and art shows. It's an effervescent spot for a taste of Brisbane's creative talent, be it offbeat, quirky, fringe, progressive or just downright weird. The on-site gallery hosts thought-provoking temporary art exhibitions and associated artist talks. See the website for upcoming exhibitions, performances and special events. (☏07-3002 7100; www.metroarts.com.au; Level 2, 109 Edward St; ⏰gallery 10am-4.30pm Mon-Fri, 2-4.30pm Sat, performance times vary; 🚢Eagle St Pier, 🚉Central)

QUT Gardens Theatre

THEATRE

32 ⭐ Map p26, D7

Despite the theatre's location on a city university campus, productions here are anything but amateur. Expect to see some of Australia's best professional stage actors here. (☎07-3138 4455; www.gardenstheatre.qut.edu.au; 2 George St, Queensland University of Technology; ◷box office 10am-4pm Mon-Fri; ♨QUT Gardens Point, ☒Central)

Paddo Tavern
COMEDY

33 ⭐ Map p26, A3

If a car wash married its supermarket cousin, their first-born would probably look like this ugly Paddington pub, which has incongruously adopted a pseudo Wild West theme inside. But it's one of the best places in Brisbane to see stand-up comedy: check the website for listings. (☎07-3369 4466; www.standup.com.au; 186 Given Tce, Paddington; ◷pub 10am-late, comedy shows vary; ☒375)

Shopping

Noosa Chocolate Factory
FOOD

34 🔒 Map p26, B4

Don't delude yourself: the small-batch, artisanal chocolates from this Sunshine Coast Willy Wonka will override any self-control. Best sellers include generous, marshmallowy Rocky Road and a very Queensland concoction of unroasted macadamias covered in Bowen mango–flavoured chocolate. Best of all, the chocolate doesn't contain palm oil. A second branch at No 156 also serves speciality coffee and hot chocolate. (www.noosachocolate factory.com.au; 144 Adelaide St; ◷8am-7pm Mon-Thu, to 9pm Fri, 9am-6pm Sat, 10am-5pm Sun; ☒Central)

Maiocchi
FASHION & ACCESSORIES

35 Map p26, C4

Home-grown label Maiocchi is well known for its gorgeous, vintage-inspired frocks, simple in cut but rich in little details and quirks. Expect custom prints, '50s silhouettes and the Japanese influences. Your next summery cocktail dress aside, the boutique also stocks tops, pants and shoes, as well as a thoughtfully curated selection of Australian-made jewellery, bags and homewares. You'll find it in the heritage-listed Brisbane Arcade. (☎07-3012 9640; www.maiocchi. com.au; Brisbane Arcade, 117 Adelaide St; ◷9am-5.30pm Mon-Thu, 8.30am-8pm Fri, 9am-4pm Sat, 11am-4pm Sun; ☒Central)

Archives Fine Books
BOOKS

36 🔒 Map p26, C5

Rickety bookshelves and squeaky floorboards set a nostalgic scene at this sprawling repository of pre-loved pages. While the true number of books on offer is a little less than the one million claimed (our little secret), the place is a veritable sea of engaging titles. The oldest book on our last visit – by the canonised Roberto Francesco Romolo Bellarmino – dated back to 1630. (☎07-3221 0491; www.archivesfine books.com.au; 40 Charlotte St; ◷9am-6pm Mon-Thu, to 7pm Fri, to 5pm Sat; ☒Central)

Folio Books BOOKS

37 🔒 Map p26, D5

Bibliophiles flock to Folio for an eclectic, sophisticated collection of titles covering everything from Canberra politics and Queensland modernism, to international art, gastronomy, design and fiction. Staff are helpful, and the place is utterly dangerous for those skilled at losing track of time. (☎07-3210 0500; www.foliobooks.com.au; 133 Mary St; ⊗8.30am-6pm Mon-Thu, to 7pm Fri, to 5pm Sat, 10am-4pm Sun; 🚢Eagle St Pier, 🚆Central)

Finders Keepers Markets MARKET

38 🔒 Map p26, E1

A biannual market with more than 100 art and design stalls held in a 19th-century museum that's now a concert hall in inner-suburban Bowen Hills. Complete with live music and food, it's a great spot to score high-quality, one-off fashion pieces, jewellery and more from local and interstate design talent. (www.thefinderskeepers.com/brisbane-markets; Old Museum, 480 Gregory Tce, Bowen Hills; adult/child $2/free; ⊗hours vary; 🚌370, 375, 🚆Fortitude Valley)

Local Life
Record Exchange

Some of the city's best retail experiences are hidden up flights of stairs or in arcades. Shop for obscure albums and rock memorabilia at sneaky **Record Exchange** (Map p26, B4; ☎07-3229 4923; www.therecordexchange.com.au; Level 1, 65 Adelaide St; ⊗9am-5pm Mon-Thu, to 9pm Fri, 9.30am-5pm Sat, 10am-4pm Sun; 🚆Central), jam-packed with an astounding collection of vinyl, CDs, DVDs and posters.

Dogstar FASHION & ACCESSORIES

39 🔒 Map p26, A3

There's more than a touch of Japanese style evident at this home-grown women's boutique. Beautiful fabrics, sculptural elements and fine details feature prominently in skirts, jackets, wraps, tunics and jewellery, creating a look that is chic, striking and bohemian spirited. (☎07-3368 2233; www.dogstar.com.au; 2 Latrobe Tce, Paddington; ⊗10am-5pm Mon-Fri, to 4pm Sat, to 3pm Sun; 🚌375)

Top Sights
D'Aguilar National Park

Getting There

🚌 **Bus** The park is 10km northwest of the city centre. Catch bus 385 ($5.70, 25 minutes) from Roma St Station to the park visitor centre; the last bus back to the city is at 4.48pm.

Suburban malaise? Slake your wilderness cravings at this roughly 36,000-hectare national park. It's just 10km northwest of the city centre yet worlds away, with cooler climate, walking trails and wildlife-watching opportunities. The park features subtropical rainforest and eucalypt forests and a wide range of bird life and native forest animals. The mountainous landscape offers a cool escape from the coast as well as lookouts offering panoramic views out to Moreton Bay.

Paradise riflebird, D'Aguilar National Park

The Park

D'Aguilar National Park is divided into two sections: the southern section is where you'll find the Walkabout Creek Discovery Centre, starting point for some of the park's best short walks. Further north is the Mount Mee section, home to two formal camp sites.

Hiking & Biking

Walking trails in the park range from a few hundred metres to a 24km-long loop. Among them is the 6km-return Morelia Track at Manorina day-use area and the 4.3km Greenes Falls Track at Mt Glorious.

Camping

D'Aguilar has two vehicle-accessible **camp sites** (☎137 468; www.npsr.qld.gov.au/parks/daguilar/camping.html; per person/family $6.15/24.60), as well as eight remote, walk-in only bush camps, allowing you to truly escape from the city for the night. The two formal camping areas are at Neurum Creek and Archer in the Mount Mee section of the park. Both have basic toilets, untreated water and fireplaces. The bush camps in the southern section are limited to a water tank. Bring in all drinking water, food, cooking stoves, camping gear and rubbish bags. Take out everything!

Mt Coot-tha Reserve & Lookout

South of D'Aguilar and only a 15-minute drive west of Brisbane CBD, **Mt Coot-tha Reserve** (www.brisbane.qld.gov.au; Mt Coot-tha Rd, Mt Coot-tha; admission free; ☉24hr; ☐471) is a huge swathe of bushland with the **Brisbane Botanic Gardens** (☎07-3403 2535; www.brisbane.qld.gov.au/botanicgardens; admission free; ☉8am-5.30pm, to 5pm Apr-Aug; ☐471) and superb panoramic **lookout** (☎07-3369 9922; www.brisbanelookout.com; 1012 Sir Samuel Griffith Dr; ☉24hr; ☐471).

---

www.nprsr.qld.gov.au/parks/daguilar

60 Mount Nebo Rd, The Gap

☑ Top Tips

At the park entrance the **Walkabout Creek Discovery Centre** (☎07-3164 3600; www.walkaboutcreek.com.au; 60 Mount Nebo Rd, The Gap; wildlife centre adult/child/family $7.20/3.50/18.25; ☉9am-4.30pm) has maps and information. Also here is the South East Queensland Wildlife Centre, where you can see a resident platypus, plus turtles, lizards, pythons and gliders.

✕ Take a Break

There are a number of picnic areas and viewpoints scattered around the park. Pack a picnic and relax! There's also a cafe and a small walk-through aviary in the Walkabout Creek Discovery Centre at the park entrance.

Explore

South Bank

While Brisbane's CBD obsesses with trade and governance, cross-river South Bank dedicates itself to cultural institutions and the finer things in life. Adding a deep shade of green are the South Park Parklands, a riverside oasis of beachside lounging and weekend market stalls. West End is an enclave of cool, laced with arty cafes, indie bookshops, microbreweries and music venues.

The Sights in a Day

☀ While South Bank is all about major sights, West End's forte is its eclectic street life, bars, shops and live music. Start in the former, crossing over from central Brisbane on the striking Kurilpa Bridge. A quick walk away are the epic murals of the **Pillars Project** (p52). Once you've decided on your favourite head back to the riverfront and spend an hour or two exploring the stellar **Gallery of Modern Art** (p44). Next door is the architecturally intriguing State Library of Queensland, while next to it is the **Queensland Art Gallery** (p53), GOMA's more traditional sibling.

☀ Consider lunching at **Gauge** (p55) or **Julius** (p55), then take a post-prandial stroll at the nearby **South Bank Parklands** (p46). Recharged, head southwest to Boundary and Vulture Sts, the buzzing heart of West End. Soak up the neighbourhood's alternative vibe, browsing books, indie comics and crates of cult-status records.

☾ If you just can't face leaving, don't. West End's bounty of eateries, bars and live-music venues will keep you humming well into the evening. Drop into **Blackstar Coffee Roasters** (p49) or **Catchment Brewing Co** (p49) for a local libation.

For a local's day in the West End, see p48.

◉ Top Sights
Gallery of Modern Art (p44)

South Bank Parklands (p46)

◯ Local Life
West End Walk (p48)

♥ Best of Brisbane & the Gold Coast

Eating
Gauge (p55)

Stokehouse Q (p56)

Morning After (p54)

Drinking
Maker (p57)

Cobbler (p58)

Getting There

🚆 **Train** Alight at South Brisbane for South Bank's major cultural institutions. South Bank Station is best for the Maritime Museum.

🚌 **Bus** Rte 199 connects Boundary St in West End to South Bank, central Brisbane, Fortitude Valley, New Farm and Teneriffe.

⛴ **Boat** CityCat services stop at South Bank 1 and 2 ferry terminal at South Bank Parklands, as well as the West End ferry terminal. CityHopper ferries stop at South Bank 3 and Maritime Museum ferry terminals.

Top Sights
Gallery of Modern Art

Enviably cool, young and occasionally irreverent, Brisbane's Gallery of Modern Art (GOMA) is the Queensland Art Gallery's hipper sibling. Since opening in 2006, the $290-million centre has established itself as one of Australia's hottest public art galleries, serving up a year-round program of thrilling, often bar-raising exhibitions showcasing some of the most intriguing creative talent in Australia and beyond.

GOMA

⊙ Map p50, E1

www.qagoma.qld.gov.au

Stanley Pl, South Bank

admission free

⊙10am-5pm

🚢South Bank Terminals 1 & 2, 🚊South Brisbane

GOMA Turns 10 installation view of *Sugar Spin: you, me, art and everything*, January 2017

Exhibitions

Exhibitions at GOMA are a mix of blockbuster shows and smaller exhibitions showcasing works from the gallery's ever-expanding permanent collection of painting, sculpture, video art, photography and installation art. The latter's cachet includes numerous works by Pablo Picasso, including *La Belle Hollandaise* (1905), one of his most lauded early paintings. It also includes major video installations by the likes of William Kentridge and Mika Rottenberg, as well as works by regional luminaries such as Ai Weiwei, Xu Bing, Nam June Paik and Queensland-born photographer and video artist Tracey Moffatt.

Cinémathèque

One of GOMA's lesser-known fortes is its purpose-built Australian Cinémathèque, an in-house film centre offering a sharply curated program of rare and classic films thematically linked to the gallery's exhibitions. Offerings include both local and international works by cult-status filmmakers, as well as rare 35mm prints, recent restorations and silent films with live musical accompaniment. Best of all, most screenings are free. Films and screening times are listed on the GOMA website.

Architecture

GOMA's star power extends to its landmark look. Primarily the work of Sydney-based Queensland architects Lindsay and Kerry Clare (of the firm Architectus), the building delivers an attention-grabbing interpretation of 20th-century International Style and vernacular tropical architecture. One of Brisbane's most striking examples of early-21st-century architecture, the pavilion-like building saw Architectus win the Australian Institute of Architects' National Award for Public Architecture in 2007.

☑ Top Tips

▶ For greater insight into the artworks, join one of GOMA's free guided tours.

▶ To avoid the crowds, head in after 2pm on weekdays, usually the quietest time at GOMA.

▶ For inspired gifts – including locally designed jewellery – drop into the well-stocked gallery shop on the ground floor.

▶ Toddler Tuesday is a free weekly program of activities, games and storytelling designed to engage toddlers with art. Book ahead on the website.

✗ Take a Break

The gallery is home to two quality eateries – GOMA Restaurant (p57) and the more casual, indoor-outdoor **GOMA Cafe Bistro** (☎07-3842 9906; lunch $15-34; ⏱10am-3pm Mon-Fri, from 8.30am Sat & Sun). The cafe serves high-quality burgers, salads and modern bistro mains, with both breakfast and lunch served on the weekends.

Top Sights
South Bank Parklands

Looking out at central Brisbane from across the river, South Bank Parklands are the city's communal backyard. It's a thriving hang-out for both locals and visitors, all of whom head in for the spectacular skyline view, beautifully landscaped spaces and the string of attractions, from regular free entertainment to a giant Ferris wheel and an oh-so-tropical artificial beach.

👁 Map p50, F3

www.visitbrisbane.com.au

Grey St, South Bank

admission free

🕐 dawn-dusk

🚢 South Bank Terminals 1, 2 & 3, 🚉 South Brisbane, South Bank

Wheel of Brisbane

Streets Beach

Squint hard enough and you might believe you're on an island in the Whitsundays. In reality, you're soaking up rays on Australia's only artificial, inner-city beach. Streets Beach is the star attraction at South Bank Parklands, a crescent-shaped, lagoon-style pool complete with gleaming white sand, crystal-clear waters, swaying palm trees and shady shallows. It's a family-friendly affair, with lifeguards and a dedicated Aquativity area for splash-happy kids. It's also a handy, free spot to cool down if your Brisbane pad doesn't have a pool.

Wheel of Brisbane

While it mightn't match the size of the Melbourne Star or London Eye, the **Wheel of Brisbane** (07-3844 3464; www.thewheelofbrisbane.com. au; Grey St, South Bank; adult/child/family $19/13.50/55; 10am-10pm Sun-Thu, to 11pm Fri & Sat; South Bank Terminals 1 & 2, South Brisbane) still manages to deliver a revealing, 360-degree panorama of the city's fast-evolving skyline. Located a few steps from the Queensland Performing Arts Centre (QPAC), the Wheel's enclosed gondolas rise to a height of nearly 60m, on a ride that lasts 10 to 12 minutes and includes audio commentary of the sights. Online bookings offer a nominal discount.

Nepalese Peace Pagoda

Standing in a rainforest grove in the shadow of the Wheel of Brisbane is South Bank's most unusual feature, the Nepalese Peace Pagoda. A replica of the Pashupatinath Temple in Kathmandu, it's a relic of World Expo 88, held on this very site back in 1988. Built over a two-year period, the pagoda is made of Terai timber from the southern jungles of Nepal, handcrafted in its entirety by 160 Nepalese families.

☑ Top Tips

▶ The Medibank Feel Good Program runs free fitness classes at South Bank Parklands throughout the year, including yoga sessions. See www.visitbrisbane. com.au for dates and times.

▶ From late September to mid-November, South Bank Parklands hosts Openair Cinemas (p60), screening big-screen classics and recent releases alfresco. Hire a beanbag or deckchair, or bring a picnic rug. Note that most sessions sell out online prior to the night of the screening, so book in advance.

✕ Take a Break

Cafes and eateries at South Bank Parklands include healthy Kiss the Berry (p55). For something more substantial, ditch the row of eateries on Stanley St for award-winning cafe-restaurant Gauge (p55) or pizza-peddling Julius (p55).

Local Life
West End Walk

The luxury apartments might be sprouting up, but West End remains Brisbane's indie-hearted hero. Hit the pavement for a robust dose of alternative cool, artistic whimsy and neighbourhood pride: a place where old-school family businesses sidle up to cult-status coffee brewers and record shops, radical comic books, craft beers, organic market stalls and off-the-radar street-art highs.

1 Davies Park Market

If it's Saturday, rise early and make a beeline for the **Davies Park Market** (www.daviesparkmarket.com.au; Davies Park; ⏰6am–2pm Sat; 🚌199, 192, 198). The neighbourhood heads here for locally grown fruit and vegetables, fresh seafood, gourmet sausages and more. Look out for the food van selling breakfast egg rolls, and pair it with a coffee from the Gypsy Vardo caravan.

Bands usually play beside the caravan from mid-morning.

② Fintan Magee Mural

Brisbane-raised Fintan Magee (dubbed the 'Australian Banksy') is known across the globe for his whimsical street art, his creations adorning walls from Melbourne to Kiev. This particularly animated West End **mural** (126 Hardgrave Rd; ☐ 198, 199) features a skulk of wild foxes, moving nimbly across a beige brick wall. It's rather apt given the number of foxes roaming suburban streets at night.

③ Blackstar Coffee Roasters

Just off Vulture St, **Blackstar Coffee Roasters** (www.blackstarcoffee.com.au; 44 Thomas St; ⊙ 7am-5pm; 🛜; ☐ 199) personifies West End spirit: indie, arty and totally laid-back. Here, superlative, locally roasted coffee is served without the hipster attitude. The crowd itself is expectantly eclectic, made up of writers, musos, nomads and coffee nerds. The top drink here is icy, cold-pressed coffee, tailor-made for those sticky Brisbane days.

④ Jet Black Cat Music

More than just a super-cool record store, **Jet Black Cat Music** (☎ 0419 571 299; www.facebook.com/jetblackcatmusic; 72 Vulture St; ⊙ 10.30am-5pm Tue-Fri, 10am-4pm Sat; ☐ 199) is a de facto lounge room for boho West Enders. Step

inside and you'll usually find a group of regulars kicking back with owner Shannon Logan, talking bands, gigs and neighbourhood gossip. Expect to be drawn into the conversation, which usually leads to passionate local recommendations and tips.

⑤ Junky Comics

West End's counterculture tendencies extend to **Junky Comics** (☎ 07-3846 5456; www.junkycomicsbrisbane.com; 93 Vulture St; ⊙ 10am-5.30pm Tue-Fri, to 5pm Sat, to 4pm Sun; ☐ 199), an independent comic-book shop opened by Brisbane-based illustrator Vlada Edirippulige (aka Junky). Drop by to browse an out-of-the-box booty of comics, from household names including Marvel and DC, to retro feminist cartoons and local zines. You'll also find limited-edition prints by local and international artists, as well as graphic tees.

⑥ Catchment Brewing Co

If it's beer o'clock, pit stop at **Catchment Brewing Co** (☎ 07-3846 1701; www.catchmentbrewingco.com.au; 150 Boundary St; ⊙ 4-10pm Mon, 11am-10pm Tue-Thu & Sun, 11am-1am Fri & Sat; ☐ 199) on West End's main strip. Run by two old friends and their families, the two-level bar and bistro brews its own suds, as well as serving a rotating cast of craft brews from other makers. Hang out in the street-art-pimped courtyard or try for one of the two small balconies.

MILTON

A B C D

1

Coronation Dr

Go Between
Bridge

Brisbane River

Montague Rd

2 The Pillars
Project

Peel St

Riverside Dr

Merivale St

2

Boundary St

Peel St

Cordelia St

Montague Rd

Norfolk Rd

Melbourne St

Donkin St

⊗13

Manning St

Anthony St

3

Mollison St

SOUTH
BRISBANE

Musgrave St

Urban
7 Climb

Russell St

Jane St

Boundary St

⊕18

Davies
Park

Wilson St

⊕22

Musgrave
Park

Montague Rd

Jane St

26⊕

⊕21

4

⊗11

Browning St

⊗8

31🔒

🔒35

Edmondstone St

Vulture St

33🔒

⊕25

WEST
END

19🔒

Besant St

⊗⊗9

Vulture St

14

⊕
20

5

Skinner St

Hardgrave Rd

Turin St

Exeter St

Cambridge St

Princhester St

Thomas St

Boundary St

Sussex St

Franklin St

Gallery of Modern Art
16

State Library of Queensland

Stanley Pl

Grey St

Queensland Cultural Centre 1

Queensland Museum & Sciencentre 3

Queensland Art Gallery 4

Victoria Bridge

North Quay

Pacific Mwy

William St

For reviews see

◉	Top Sights	p44
◉	Sights	p52
✕	Eating	p54
🍷	Drinking	p57
★	Entertainment	p59
🛍	Shopping	p61

N   0 ————— 400 m
    0 ————— 0.2 miles

12
17

Melbourne St

Fish La

23

South Brisbane

Grey St

Wheel of Brisbane

10

Brisbane River

River City Cruises 6

South Bank Parklands

City Hopper Ferry

28

32

27

Suncorp Piazza

24

SOUTH BANK

Glenelg St

Merivale St

Cordelia St

Ernest St

29

Colchester St

Ernest St

Grey St

Little Stanley St

30 34

i

City Cat Ferry

Goodwill Bridge

Pacific Mwy

Tribune St

Gladstone Rd

Vulture St

South Bank

Sidon St

South Bank Parklands

Queensland Maritime Museum 5

15

Sights

Queensland Cultural Centre

CULTURAL CENTRE

 1 ⊙ Map p50, E1

On South Bank, just over Victoria Bridge from the CBD, the Queensland Cultural Centre is the epicentre of Brisbane's cultural confluence. Surrounded by subtropical gardens, the sprawling complex of architecturally notable buildings includes the Queensland Performing Arts Centre (p59), the Queensland Museum & Sciencentre, the Queensland Art Gallery, the State Library of Queensland, and the particularly outstanding Gallery of Modern Art (GOMA). (Melbourne St, South Bank; 🚢 South Bank Terminals 1 & 2, 🚆 South Brisbane)

☑ Top Tip

For Kids

South Bank is home to numerous free, child-friendly attractions, including Streets Beach, Queensland Museum, Queensland Art Gallery and the Gallery of Modern Art (p44). The latter is home to a dedicated Children's Art Centre, with interactive exhibitions and craft activities. On Friday from 5.30pm, the Queensland Performing Arts Centre (p59) hosts its family-friendly Green Jam sessions, with street food and free live music.

The Pillars Project

PUBLIC ART

 2 ⊙ Map p50, D1

Beneath the South Brisbane rail overpass, a handful of concrete pillars have been transformed into giant street-art murals by some of the hottest names on the scene. Especially notable is Iceland-based Guido Van Helten's arresting portrait of an Aboriginal child, as well as Fintan Magee's portrait of a man in rising floodwaters, holding a child afloat on a boogie board. The latter work is both a symbol of hope and a tribute to the floods that devastated the region in 2011. (www.thepillarsproject.com; Merrivale St, South Brisbane; ⊙24hr; 🚌198, 🚢South Bank Terminals 1 & 2, 🚆South Brisbane)

Queensland Museum & Sciencentre

MUSEUM

3 ⊙ Map p50, E2

Dig deeper into Queensland history at the state's main historical repository, where intriguing exhibits include a skeleton of the state's own dinosaur Muttaburrasaurus (aka 'Mutt'), and the *Avian Cirrus*, the tiny plane in which Queenslander Bert Hinkler made the first England-to-Australia solo flight in 1928. Also on-site is the Sciencentre, an educational fun house with a plethora of interactive exhibits delving into life science and technology. Expect long queues during school holidays. (📞07-3840 7555; www.southbank.qm.qld.gov.au; cnr Grey & Melbourne Sts, South Bank; Queensland Museum admission free, Sciencentre adult/

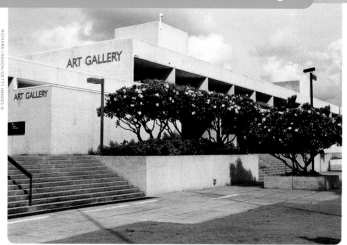

RICHARD I ANSON/GETTY IMAGES ©

Queensland Art Gallery

child/family $14.50/11.50/44.50; ⊙9.30am-5pm; ⛴South Bank Terminals 1 & 2, ☒South Brisbane)

Queensland Art Gallery   GALLERY

4 ◎ Map p50, E2

While current construction works (due for completion in September 2017) have temporarily limited its gallery space, QAG is home to a fine permanent collection of Australian and international works. Australian art dates from the 1840s to the 1970s: check out works by celebrated masters including Sir Sidney Nolan, Arthur Boyd, William Dobell and Albert Namatjira. (QAG; www.qagoma.qld.gov.au;

Melbourne St, South Bank; admission free; ⊙10am-5pm; ⛴South Bank Terminals 1 & 2, ☒South Brisbane)

Queensland Maritime Museum   MUSEUM

5 ◎ Map p50, H5

On the southern edge of the South Bank Parklands is this sea-salty museum, the highlight of which is the gigantic HMAS *Diamantina*, a restored WWII frigate that you can clamber aboard and explore. (⌖07-3844 5361; www.maritimemuseum.com.au; Stanley St; adult/child/family $16/7/38; ⊙9.30am-4.30pm, last admission 3.30pm; ⛴Maritime Museum, ☒South Bank)

River City Cruises CRUISE

6 Map p50, F2

River City runs 1½-hour cruises with commentary from South Bank to New Farm and back. They depart from South Bank at 10.30am and 12.30pm (plus 2.30pm during summer). (☏ 0428 278 473; www.rivercitycruises.com. au; South Bank Parklands Jetty A; adult/child/family $29/15/65)

Urban Climb CLIMBING

7 Map p50, B3

A large indoor climbing wall with one of the largest bouldering walls in Australia. Suitable for both beginners and advanced climbing geeks.

(☏ 07-3844 2544; www.urbanclimb. au; 2/220 Montague Rd, West End; adult/child $20/18, once-off registration fee $5; ⊙ noon-10pm Mon-Fri, 10am-6pm Sat & Sun; 🚍 60, 192, 198)

Eating

Plenty West End CAFE $

8 Map p50, A4

In the far west of West End lies this graphics-factory-turned-cafe, a rustic, industrial backdrop for farm-to-table edibles. Scan the counter for freshly made panini and cakes, or the blackboard for headliners such as caramelised Brussels sprouts with pumpkin purée, feta, raisins and pumpkin seeds. Libations include fresh juices, kombucha on tap and fantastic, organic coffee. When you're done, pick up some pineapple hot sauce at the in-store providore. (☏ 07-3255 3330; www. facebook.com/plentywestend; 284 Montague Rd, West End; dishes $5.50-23.50; ⊙ 6.30am-3pm, kitchen closes 2.25pm; 🛜 🍽; 🚍 60, 192, 198)

Morning After CAFE $

9 Map p50, B5

Decked out in contemporary blonde-wood furniture, gleaming subway tiles and bold green accents, this new-school West End cafe is crisper than an apple. Join the effortlessly cool for vibrant, revamped cafe fare such as zucchini fritters with fried eggs, carrot and ginger purée and Vietnamese

Queensland Museum & Sciencentre (p52)

salad, and bucatini pasta with kale pesto, spinach purée and pistachio. Alas, the coffee is a little less consistent. (☑07-3844 0500; www.morningafter.com.au; cnr Vulture & Cambridge Sts, West End; breakfast $9-19, lunch mains $15-21; ⏰7am-4pm; 🛜📷; 🚌199)

Kiss the Berry

HEALTH FOOD $

 10   Map p50, F3

Overlooking South Bank Parklands is this youthful, upbeat açaí bar serving fresh, tasty bowls of the organic super-food in various combinations. Our favourite is the naughty-but-nice Snickers Delight (with banana, strawberries, raw cacao powder, peanut butter, coconut water, almond milk, granola, raw cocoa nibs and coconut yoghurt and flakes). For a liquid açaí fix, opt for one of the meal-in-a-cup smoothies. (☑07-3846 6128; www.kisstheberry.com; 65/114 Grey St, South Bank; bowls $10.50-16; ⏰7am-5pm; 📷; 🚢South Bank Terminals 1 & 2, 🚌South Brisbane)

Beach Burrito Company

MEXICAN $

11   Map p50, C4

Beach-shack style and a predictable Mex repertoire of tacos, burritos, quesadillas and margaritas. (☑07-3846 6286; www.beachburritocompany.com; 100 Boundary St, West End; mains $12-21; ⏰11.30am-10pm Sun-Thu, to 10pm Fri & Sat; 🚌198, 199)

⬤ Local Life
High Tea

Ladies who lunch, brides-to-be and general bon vivants have a particular soft spot for high tea at South Bank's **Bacchus** (Map p50, E3; ☑07-3364 0837; www.bacchussouthbank.com.au; Rydges South Bank, 9 Glenelg St, South Brisbane; high tea $38, with glass of champagne from $53; ⏰high tea 2.30-4.30pm Tue-Thu & Sun, 1.30-4.30pm Fri & Sat; 🚢South Bank Terminals 1 & 2, 🚌South Brisbane).

Gauge

MODERN AUSTRALIAN $$

12   Map p50, E2

All-day, cafe-style Gauge is so hot right now. In a crisp, sparse space punctuated by black-spun aluminium lamps, native flora and a smashing wine list, clean, contemporary dishes burst with Australian confidence. Signatures include a provocative 'blood taco' packed with roasted bone marrow, mushroom and native thyme, and a brilliant twist on banana bread – garlic bread with burnt vanilla and brown butter. (☑07-3852 6734; www.gaugebrisbane.com.au; 77 Grey St, South Brisbane; breakfast $12-19, mains $26-33; ⏰7am-3pm Mon-Wed, 7am-3pm & 5.30-9pm Thu & Fri, 8am-3pm & 5.30-9pm Sat, 8am-3pm Sun; 🚢South Bank Terminals 1 & 2, 🚌South Brisbane)

Julius

ITALIAN $$

Suited up in polished concrete and the orange glow of Aperol, this svelte Italian (see 12 Map p50, E2) fires up superlative pizzas, divided into *pizze rosse* (with tomato sauce) or *pizze bianche* (without). The former includes a simple, beautiful marinara, cooked the proper Neapolitan way (sans seafood). The pasta dishes are also solid, with *fritelle di ricotta* (fried ricotta dumplings filled with custard) making a satisfying epilogue. (☏07-3844 2655; www.juliuspizzeria.com.au; 77 Grey St, South Brisbane; pizzas $21-24.50; ☉noon-9.30pm Sun, Tue & Wed, to 10pm Thu, to 10.30pm Fri & Sat; ⛴South Bank Terminals 1 & 2, ⛿South Brisbane)

Billykart West End

13   Map p50, C3   MODERN AUSTRALIAN $$

Brisbane-based celeb chef Ben O'Donoghue heads Billykart, a slick yet casual eatery where billykart blueprints and faux Queenslander veneers salute local childhood memories. Dishes are beautifully textured and flavoured, from the cult-status breakfast Aussie-Asian eggs (tiger prawn, bacon, deep-fried egg, oyster sauce, chilli and shizu cress) to a smashing lunch-and-dinner spanner crab spaghettini. Weekend breakfast is especially popular; head in by 9am. (☏07-3177 9477; www.billykart.com.au; 2 Edmondstone St, West End; breakfast $6-23.50, dinner mains $26-36; ☉restaurant 7am-2.30pm Mon & Sun, 7am-9.30pm Tue-Sat, shop 11am-5pm Mon, 11am-9pm Tue-Fri, 9am-9pm Sat, 9am-5pm Sun; ⛿192, 196, 198, 199)

Sea Fuel

14   Map p50, B5   FISH & CHIPS $$

The only thing missing is a beach at Sea Fuel, one of Brisbane's best fish-and-chip peddlers. It's a polished, modern spot, with distressed timber tabletops and blown-up photos of coastal scenes. The fish is fresh and sustainably caught in Australian and New Zealand waters, and the golden chips flawlessly crisp and sprinkled with chicken salt. Alternatives include fresh oysters, Thai fish cakes and sprightly salads. (☏07-3844 9473; www. facebook.com/seafuel; 57 Vulture St, West End; meals $14-26; ☉11.30am-8.30pm; ♿; ⛿199)

Stokehouse Q

15   Map p50, H5   MODERN AUSTRALIAN $$$

Sophisticated Stokehouse guarantees a dizzying high, its confident, locally sourced menu paired with utterly

Local Life
Little Greek Taverna

Up-tempo, eternally busy and in a prime West End location, the **Little Greek Taverna** (Map p50, C3; ☏07-3255 2215; www.littlegreektaverna.com.au; 5/1 Browning St, West End; mains $15-17, banquets per person $35-45; ☉11am-9pm Tue-Sun; ⛿196, 198, 199) is a solid spot for Hellenic feasting and people watching. Launch into a prawn and saganaki salad or a classic lamb gyros (souvlaki), washed down with thick, sucker-punch Greek coffee.

GOMA Cafe Bistro (p45)

gorgeous river and city views. At crisp, linen-clad tables, urbanites toast to inspired creations such as chicken liver and Madeira brûlée with fruit toast, pear and native cranberry chutney. Next door, Stoke Bar offers similar views for a more casual (albeit pricey) drinking session. (☑07-3020 0600; www.stokehouse.com.au; River Quay, Sidon St, South Bank; mains $36-42; ⏱noon-late Mon-Thu, 11am-late Fri-Sun; ⛴South Bank Terminal 3, ⧀South Bank)

GOMA Restaurant

MODERN AUSTRALIAN $$$

16 🍴 Map p50, E1

Located at the Gallery of Modern Art, this high-end, two-hatted restaurant showcases native ingredients in sophisticated, contemporary dishes. Wines focus on the New World, with a special emphasis on Queensland and maverick winemakers. (☑07-3842 9916; www.qagoma.qld.gov.au; Gallery of Modern Art, Stanley Pl, South Bank; mains $39-47; ⏱noon-2pm Wed-Sun, plus 5.30-8pm Fri; ⛴South Bank Terminals 1 & 2, ⧀South Brisbane)

Drinking

Maker

COCKTAIL BAR

17 🍸 Map p50, E2

Intimate, black-clad and spliced by a sexy brass bar, Maker crafts seamless, seasonal cocktails using house liqueurs, out-of-the-box ingredients and a splash of whimsy. Here, classic negronis are made with house-infused vermouth, while gin and tonics get Australian with native quandong and finger lime. Other fortes include a sharp edit of boutique wines by the glass and beautiful bar bites prepared with award-winning restaurant Gauge (p55). (☎0437 338 072; 9 Fish Lane, South Brisbane; ⏰4pm-midnight Tue-Sun; 🚊South Bank Terminals 1 & 2, 🚉South Brisbane)

Cobbler   BAR

18 🚇 Map p50, C4

Whisky fans will weep tears of joy at the sight of Cobbler's imposing bar, graced with more than 400 whiskies from around the globe. Channelling

a speakeasy vibe, this dimly lit West End wonder also pours a cogno-scenti selection of rums, tequilas and liqueurs, not to mention a crafty selection of cocktails that add modern twists to the classics. Bottoms up! (www.cobblerbar.com; 7 Browning St, West End; ⏰5pm-1am Mon, 4pm-1am Tue-Thu & Sun, 4pm-2am Fri & Sat; 🚌60, 192, 198, 199)

Jungle   BAR

19 🚇 Map p50, C5

Aloha and welcome to paradise... Well, at least to Brisbane's only proper tiki bar. An intimate, hand-built bamboo hideaway pimped with wood-carved stools, a green-glowing bar and DJ-spun Hawaiian tunes, it's an apt place to cool down with a tropical libation.

Lychee Lounge

RICHARD I'ANSON/GETTY IMAGES ©

Keep it classic with a rumalicious piña colada (served in a pineapple, naturally), or neck a Red Stripe lager from Jamaica. (📞0449 568 732; www.facebook.com/junglewestend; 76 Vulture St, West End; 🕙noon-midnight Thu-Sun; 🚌199)

The End BAR

20 Map p50, C5

Hipsters, mocha stout and Morrissey on the turntable: this former Trash Video store is now a loud, brooding hang-out for indie-centric West Enders. Entertainment comes in the form of top local DJs, bands and solo artists. (📞07-3846 6862; 1/73 Vulture St, West End; 🕙3pm-midnight; 🚌199)

Archive Beer Boutique BAR

21 🍺 Map p50, C4

A foaming juggernaut, Archive serves up a dizzying choice of craft suds. Whether you're hankering for a Brisbane chilli-choc porter, a Melbourne American IPA or a Sydney guava gose, chances are you'll find it pouring here. There are more than 20 rotating beers on tap, as well as hundreds of Aussie and imported bottled brews. Decent bar grub includes grilled meats, burgers and pizzas. (📞07-3844 3419; www.archivebeerboutique.com.au; 100 Boundary St, West End; 🕙11am-late; 🚌198, 199)

Lychee Lounge COCKTAIL BAR

22 🍸 Map p50, C4

Sink into the lush furniture at this moody, opium-den-inspired cocktail lounge, where lemon myrtle and Tasmanian amaro give negronis a local accent, and where absinthe and apple liqueur join forces with fresh apple juice, lime and rosemary in a sucker-punch Tai Kwan Do. The Asian design motif extends to the bites, which sees Med-style plates hobnobbing with taro chips and barramundi and shallot money bags. (📞07-3846 0544; www.lycheelounge.com.au; 2/94 Boundary St, West End; 🕙3pm-midnight Sun-Thu, to 1am Fri & Sat; 🚌198, 199, 196)

Entertainment

Queensland Performing Arts Centre PERFORMING ARTS

23 ⭐ Map p50, F2

Brisbane's main performing arts centre comprises four venues and a small exhibition space focused on aspects of the performing arts. The centre's busy calendar includes ballet, concerts, theatre and comedy, from both Australian and international acts. One-hour backstage tours run on Friday from 10.30am; book tickets by phone or email, or purchase them on the day from the ground-floor QPAC cafe. (QPAC; 📞guided tours 07-3840 7444, tickets 136 246; www.qpac.com.au; Queensland Cultural Centre, cnr Grey & Melbourne Sts, South Bank; tours adult/child $15/10; 🕙box office 9am-8.30pm Mon-Sat; 🚢South Bank Terminals 1 & 2, 🚉South Brisbane)

Ben & Jerry's Openair Cinemas CINEMA

24 ⭐ Map p50, F3

From late September to mid-November you can watch big-screen classics and recent releases under the stars (or clouds) at the Rainforest Green at South Bank Parklands. Hire a beanbag or deckchair, or bring a picnic rug. Note that most sessions sell out online prior to the night of the screening, so book in advance. Live music (which sometimes includes prolific Australian acts) runs beforehand. (www. openaircinemas.com.au; Rainforest Green, South Bank Parklands, South Bank; adult/child online $17/12, at the gate $22/17; ⏰from 5.30pm Tue-Sat, from 5pm Sun; 🚤South Bank Terminals 1 & 2, 🚉South Brisbane)

Lock 'n' Load LIVE MUSIC

25 ⭐ Map p50, C4

Ebullient and woody, this two-storey gastropub lures an upbeat crowd of music fans, here to watch jazz, acoustic, roots, blues and soul acts take to the small front stage. Catch a gig, then show up for breakfast or lunch the next day (the brekkie of craft-beer baked beans with fat bacon, sour cream, jalapeños and corn bread tames a hangover). Check the website for upcoming gigs. (📞07-3844 0142; www.locknloadbistro.com.au; 142 Boundary St, West End; ⏰3pm-late Mon-Thu, from noon Fri, from 7am Sat & Sun; 🛜; 🚉199)

Max Watt's House of Music LIVE MUSIC

26 ⭐ Map p50, C4

Unobstructed sight lines and an eclectic line-up of local and international talent underscore this intimate music room. Past guests include Toronto post-bop outfit BadBadNotGood, DC-based progressive metal heads Periphery and LA rapper Kid Ink. Check the website for upcoming gigs. (📞1300 762 545; www.maxwatts. com.au/brisbane; 125 Boundary St, West End; 🚉199)

Queensland Conservatorium OPERA, LIVE MUSIC

27 ⭐ Map p50, F3

Part of Griffith University, the conservatorium hosts 250 music performances a year, featuring students, faculty and alumni. It also hosts touring artists and other special events. Many concerts are free. (📞07-3735 6241; www.griffith.edu.au/music/queensland-conservatorium; 140 Grey St, South Bank; tickets $8-40; ⏰box office 7am-10pm Mon-Fri, 8am-6pm Sat & Sun; 🚤South Bank Terminals 1 & 2, 🚉South Brisbane)

Brisbane Convention & Exhibition Centre LIVE MUSIC

28 ⭐ Map p50, E3

An 8000-seat auditorium in South Bank, hosting anything from arena-style musicals to pop acts and expos.

Nepalese Peace Pagoda (p47)

(📞07-3308 3000, 1800 063 308; www.bcec.com.au; cnr Merivale & Glenelg Sts, South Bank; 🚤South Bank Terminals 1 & 2, 🚈South Brisbane)

South Bank Cineplex CINEMA

29 ⭐ Map p50, F4

The cheapest complex for mainstream releases: wade through a sea of popcorn aromas and teenagers. (📞07-3829 7970; www.cineplex.com.au; cnr Grey & Ernest Sts, South Bank; adult/child from $6.50/4.50; ⏱10am-late; 🚤South Bank Terminals 1, 2 & 3, 🚈South Bank)

Shopping

Young Designers Market MARKET

30 🔒 Map p50, G4

Explore the work of up to 80 of the city's best emerging designers and artists, selling fashion and accessories, contemporary jewellery, art, furniture and homewares. Held beside South Bank Parklands, the market generally runs on the first Sunday of the month. (www.youngdesignersmarket.com.au; Little Stanley St, South Bank; ⏱10am-4pm, 1st Sun of the month; 🚤South Bank Terminal 3, 🚈South Bank)

Where the Wild Things Are
BOOKS

31 🔒 Map p50, C4

Little brother to Avid Reader next door, Where the Wild Things Are stocks a whimsical collection of books for toddlers, older kids and teens. The bookshop also runs regular activities, from weekly story-time sessions to book launches, signings and crafty workshops covering topics such as book illustration. Scan the book-shop's website and Facebook page for upcoming events. (☎07-3255 3987; www.wherethewildthingsare.com.au; 191 Boundary St, West End; ⊙8.30am-6pm Mon-Sat, to 5pm Sun; 🚻; 🚌199)

Title
BOOKS

32 🔒 Map p50, F3

Offbeat and alternative art, cinema, music, photography and design tomes, plus vinyl, CDs and DVDs – a quality dose of subversive rebelliousness (just

---

Understand
Brisbane Festivals

Brisbane knows how to party, with a packed calendar of music, arts and sports events. Some favourites:

Brisbane Festival (www.brisbanefestival.com.au; ⊙Sep) One of Australia's largest and most diverse arts festivals, running for three weeks in September and featuring an impressive schedule of concerts, plays, dance and fringe events. The festival ends with the spectacular 'Riverfire', an elaborate fireworks show over the Brisbane River.

Brisbane Street Art Festival (www.bsafest.com.au; ⊙Feb) The hiss of spray cans underscores this booming two-week festival, which sees local and international street artists transform city walls into arresting artworks. Live mural art aside, the program includes exhibitions, music, theatre, light shows, workshops and street-art masterclasses.

Valley Fiesta (www.valleyfiesta.com; ⊙Oct) A family-friendly, three-day street party in Fortitude Valley, with free concerts and DJ sets, as well as art, fashion shows, market stalls and food.

NRL Grand Final (www.nrl.com.au; ⊙late Sep) The culmination of the annual National Rugby League competition – which features the Brisbane Broncos, North Queensland Cowboys and Gold Coast Titans among 13 other teams – is the bone-crunching Grand Final in late September. Get to a barbecue, drink some beer and yell at the TV with the locals.

what South Bank needs!). There's an especially strong jazz music section, as well as cool gift items (think tote bags with tongue-in-cheek slogans). (📞07-3844 4900; www.titlestore.com.au; 1/133 Grey St, South Bank; ⏰noon-6pm Mon, 11am-6pm Tue & Wed, 11am-7pm Thu, 10am-6pm Fri, 10am-5pm Sat, 11am-4pm Sun; 🚊South Bank Terminals 1 & 2, 🚉South Brisbane)

Avid Reader
BOOKS

33 🔒 Map p50, C4

Diverse pages, a little cafe in the corner and frequent readings and bookish events: a real West End cultural hub. (📞07-3846 3422; www.avidreader.com.au; 193 Boundary St, West End; ⏰8.30am-8.30pm Mon-Fri, to 6pm Sat, to 5pm Sun; 📶; 🚍199)

Collective Markets South Bank
MARKET

34 🔒 Map p50, G4

South Bank's Collective Markets may draw the tourist hordes, but its stalls sell some great items, including artisan leather wallets, breezy summer frocks, prints, skincare and contemporary handmade jewellery. (www.collectivemarkets.com.au; Stanley St Plaza; ⏰5-9pm Fri, 10am-9pm Sat, 9am-4pm Sun; 🚊South Bank Terminal 3, 🚉South Bank)

Collective Markets South Bank

Boundary Street Markets
MARKET

35 🔒 Map p50, C4

A compact, twice-weekly congregation of mainly food trucks and stalls dishing up anything from Japanese noodles to crispy pancakes and vegan doughnuts. Check the website for special themed events, among them vegan and kids' market days. (www.boundarystreetmarkets.com.au; 56 Russell St, West End; ⏰4-10pm Fri & Sat; 🚍199)

Explore

Fortitude Valley

Fortitude Valley is Brisbane's bad boy, a party-loving hedonist packed with thumping dance clubs, pubs and rocking music venues. Beyond the grit lies a booming, urbane mix of buzzing eateries, crafty cocktail bars and clued-in boutiques. Add to this a slew of art galleries and the heady scents of Chinatown and you have one of Brisbane's most intriguing corners.

The Sights in a Day

☀️ During daylight hours, Fortitude Valley is more about eating, shopping and gallery hopping must-see tourist sights. Start the day poking around the lavishly stocked **James Street Market** (p69) and perhaps a swim at **Valley Pool** (p67).

☀️ Head in for lunch at cheeky **Les Bubbles** (p71) before checking out the rotating exhibitions at the **Institute of Modern Art** (p69; located inside the Judith Wright Centre of Contemporary Arts; pictured left). One block further southeast on Brunswick St is the **Jan Murphy Gallery** (p69), a stalwart of the city's commercial gallery scene. At tiny Chinatown, whet the appetite at the small handful of Asian grocery stores before heading to Bakery Lane and Winn Lane, two small, Melbourne-style laneways dotted with unique boutiques and eateries. Return to James St to experience the more salubrious side of the Valley, with its polished shopping strip.

🌙 Settle in for coffee (or champers) or turn right into Robertson St for rare perfumes at **Libertine** (p67) and cutting-edge creativity at **TW Fine Art** (p67). When dusk is at the door, head back to Ann St and up 11 floors to rooftop bar **Eleven** (p73) for a sucker-punch skyline view, then bar hop your way back up Ann and Brunswick Sts.

For a local's day in Fortitude Valley, see p66.

🔍 Local Life

A Day in Fortitude Valley (p66)

💗 Best of Brisbane & the Gold Coast

Eating
King Arthur Cafe (p66)

Longtime (p71)

E'cco (p72)

Drinking & Entertainment
Gerard's Bar (p73)

Cloudland (p74)

Beat MegaClub (p77)

Shopping
Camilla (p78)

Fallow (p78)

Getting There

🚆 **Train** All six metropolitan train lines (including trains to the airport) run through Fortitude Valley Station, offering frequent services to the city and South Bank.

🚌 **Bus** Fortitude Valley is serviced by a large number of bus routes. Most city- and South Bank–bound buses run south along Ann St, while most buses heading out of the city run north along Wickham Tce. Rte 470 runs from Teneriffe ferry terminal to James and Ann Sts on its way to the city and Toowong.

Local Life
A Day in Fortitude Valley

Fortitude Valley is more than its bars, clubs and boozed-up weekend crowds. Indeed, this corner of the city is a hub for the cognoscenti, studded with gorgeous cafes, sharply curated galleries and boutiques, cool laneways and one of Brisbane's best-loved swimming spots. Head in for a morning or afternoon and savour Brisbane at its urbane best.

① King Arthur Cafe

The menu at **King Arthur Cafe** (☎07-3358 1670; www.kingarthurcafe.com; 164c Arthur St; meals $11.50-21; ⊙7am-3pm Tue-Fri, to 2pm Sat-Mon; ☎; ☒470, ☒Fortitude Valley) is famously fond of all things local. Sprout Artisan Bakery provides the bread and pastries, Coffee Supreme supplies the beans, and the jams and relishes are all made at King Arthur's sibling cafe, Merriweather in South Brisbane.

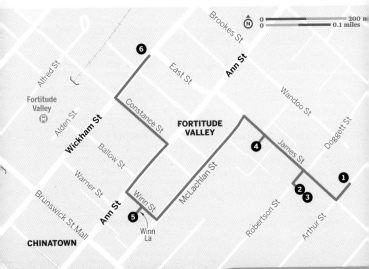

❷ TW Fine Art

In a laneway just off Robertson St is pocket rocket **TW Fine Art** (☎0437 348 755; www.twfineart.com; 181 Robertson St; ⏰10am-5pm Tue-Sat, to 3pm Sun; 🚇470, 🚉Fortitude Valley). This is one of Brisbane's more progressive private art galleries, indicative of an evolving, increasingly sophisticated city. Chances are you'll find affable owner Tove Langridge running the space, a man with a resolutely international outlook and a stable of critically acclaimed, boundary-pushing artists from Melbourne to Chicago.

❸ Libertine

On-point locals spray and sniff at **Libertine** (☎07-3216 0122; www.libertineparfumerie.com.au; 181 Robertson St; ⏰10am-5pm Mon-Fri, 9.30am-5pm Sat, 10am-4pm Sun; 🚇470, 🚉Fortitude Valley), a gorgeous little parfumerie specialising in harder-to-find, artisanal fragrances and skincare from around the world. The store also runs champagne-fuelled, one-hour perfume masterclasses several times a week.

❹ Scrumptious Reads

Enter **Scrumptious Reads** (☎07-3852 6797; www.scrumptiousreads.com.au; 5-6/19 James St; ⏰10am-5pm Mon-Sat, to 4pm Sun; 🚇470, 🚉Fortitude Valley), a small, tranquil bookshop with an emphasis on niche, in-the-know journals, magazines and travel guides, and a large communal table where you can sit, browse and sip beautifully brewed matcha tea while nibbling on suitably scrumptious cakes.

❺ Winn Lane

Tiny Winn Lane is a cul-de-sac of cool. Check out the iconic 'No Standing' stencil artwork to the right of the laneway entrance, then slip inside to shop for local jewellery at **Miss Bond** (☎0410 526 082; www.facebook.com/missbond.com.au; 5g Winn Lane; ⏰10am-4pm Wed-Sat, to 3pm Sun; 🚉Fortitude Valley) and men's accessories at **Outpost** (☎07-3666 0306; www.theoutpoststore.com.au; 5 Winn St; ⏰10am-6pm Tue-Thu & Sat, to 8pm Fri, 9.30am-4.30pm Sun; 🚉Fortitude Valley). The latter is named after a legendary rock venue around the corner, now a strip club. DJs play the laneway on Saturday afternoon.

❻ Valley Pool

When it's time to cool off, head over to the heritage-listed **Valley Pool** (www.valleypoolbrisbane.com.au; 432 Wickham St; adult/child $5.40/3.90, family from $11.50; ⏰5am-7.30pm Mon-Fri, to 6pm Fri, 5am-6pm Sat, 7.30am-6pm Sun mid-Sep–mid-Apr, 5.15am-7.30pm Mon-Thu, to 7pm Fri, to 5pm Sat, 7.30am-5pm Sun rest of year; 🚉Fortitude Valley). It's a palm-fringed, 50m affair, pulling everyone from elite swimmers to inner-city pleasure seekers of all orientations out to bronze, splash and check out the eye candy. The place is the base to the Commercial Swimming Club, known for pumping out a string of Australian Olympic champions.

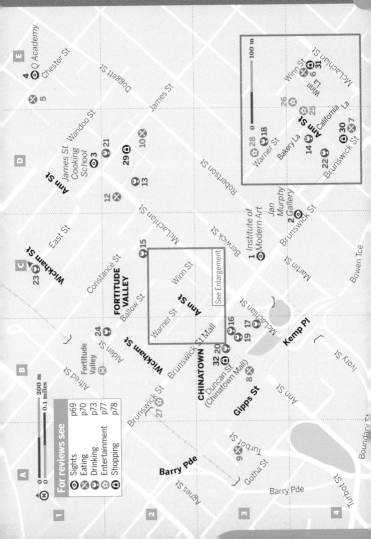

FORTITUDE VALLEY

CHINATOWN

For reviews see
⊙ Sights   p69
⊗ Eating   p70
⊗ Drinking   p73
⊕ Entertainment   p77
⊕ Shopping   p78

Sights

Institute of Modern Art   GALLERY

1 ⊙ Map p68, C3

Located inside the industrious Judith Wright Centre of Contemporary Arts (p77), the non-commercial Institute of Modern Art serves up oft-interesting exhibitions showcasing both Australian and international artists. Works span the gamut of media, from site-specific installations and photography, to painting and video art. The space also houses a decent art-themed bookshop. (IMA; ☎07-3252 5750; www.ima.org.au; 420 Brunswick St, Fortitude Valley; ⏱noon-6pm Tue, Wed, Fri & Sat, to 8pm Thu; ☒Fortitude Valley)

Jan Murphy Gallery   GALLERY

2 ⊙ Map p68, C4

Behind its strip of Astroturf, this respected gallery delivers regularly changing exhibitions of contemporary Australian art from both established and emerging talent. Expect anything from painting and sculpture to photography. (☎07-3254 1855; www.janmurphygallery.com.au; 486 Brunswick St, Fortitude Valley; ⏱10am-5pm Tue-Sat; ☒195, 196, 199, ☒Fortitude Valley)

James St Cooking School   COOKING

3 ⊙ Map p68, D1

Nurture your inner Jamie Oliver at this fantastic cooking school, aptly located above the gut-rumbling **James Street Market** (www.jamesst.com.au/james-st-market; 22 James St, Fortitude Valley; 8-piece sashimi $17, hot dishes $10-28; ⏱8.30am-7pm Mon-Fri, 8am-6pm Sat & Sun; ☒470, ☒Fortitude Valley). The school offers both hands-on and demonstration classes, its three-hour courses covering themes as varied as sausage making; Middle Eastern, Indian and Modern French cooking; even 'beer and BBQing'. Expect to play with lots of fresh produce from the market downstairs. (☎07-3252 8850; www.jamesstcookingschool.com.au; 22 James St, Fortitude Valley; 3hr class $145-160; ☒470, ☒Fortitude Valley)

Q Academy   MASSAGE

4 ⊙ Map p68, E1

Q Academy offers one of Brisbane's best bargains: one-hour relaxation or remedial massage for $30. Although the practitioners are massage students at the accredited academy, all have extensive theoretical training and enough experience to leave you feeling

---

Understand

Street Art

Fortitude Valley is a hot spot for street art in Brisbane. Good spots to get an eyeful include Winn St, Coniston Lane (behind Family nightclub), Constance St (beside the Tryp Hotel), and the wall right beside Jamie's Espresso (on the corner of James and Robertson Sts).

a lot lighter. It's a very popular spot, so book online at least a week in advance. (☎1300 204 080; www.qacademy.com.au; 20 Chester St, Newstead; 1hr massage $30; 300, 302, 305, 306, 322, 470)

Eating

Nodo Donuts

CAFE $

5 Map p68, E1

Light-washed, hip-kid Nodo serves up Brisbane's poshest doughnuts (usually sold out by 2pm), with combos like blueberry and lemon and Valrhona chocolate with beetroot. They're baked (not fried), gluten-free and even include a raw variety, dehydrated for nine hours. The rest of the cafe menu is equally focused on natural, unrefined ingredients, from the green breakfast bowl to the activated almond-milk Magic Mushroom shake. Great coffee, too. (☎07-3852 2230; www.nodo.com.au; 1 Ella St, Newstead; dishes $7.50-16; 7am-3pm Tue-Fri, from 8am Sat & Sun; ; 300, 302, 305, 306, 322, 470)

Local Life

The Foundry

The Foundry (Map p68, B2; www.thefoundry.net.au; 228 Wickham St; 5pm-5am Thu-Sun; Fortitude Valley) serves up good times in the form of pool tables, arcade games and a solid line-up of top-notch, up-and-coming Aussie bands. The joint is a proper music and arts incubator, with both rehearsal spaces and accommodation for music acts upstairs, as well as a number of in-house creative studios. Expect anything from indie acoustic pop to punk.

Ben's Burgers

BURGERS $

6 Map p68, E4

Prime ingredients drive Ben's, a small, pumping joint in the Valley's coolest laneway. Roll out of bed for a breakfast Elvis (bacon, peanut butter, banana, maple syrup), or head in later for the trio of lunch and dinner burgers, among them a meat-free option. Sides are straightforward – fries or chilli-cheese fries – with brownies and pecan pie making for a fitting epilogue. (☎07-3195 3094; www.bensburgers.com.au; Winn Lane, 5 Winn St; burgers $11; 7am-late; Fortitude Valley)

Beach Burrito Company

MEXICAN $

7 Map p68, D4

An open-fronted, shack-style Mexican chain pumping out all the street-food standards, from tacos, chimichangas and quesadillas, to burritos and churros. The courtyard out the back gets busy as a woodpecker on Friday and Saturday nights. Killer 'El Diablo' margaritas. Other branches include West End (p55). (☎07-3852 6084; www.beachburritocompany.com; 2/350 Brunswick St, Fortitude Valley; mains $12-21; 11.30am-10pm Sun-Thu, to 11pm Fri & Sat; Fortitude Valley)

Chinatown, Fortitude Valley

Longtime

THAI $$

8 Map p68, B3

Blink and you'll miss the alley leading to this dim, kicking hot spot. The menu is designed for sharing, with a banging repertoire of sucker-punch, Thai-inspired dishes that include a must-try soft-shell-crab *bao* (steamed bun) with Asian slaw. Reservations are only accepted for 5.30pm, 6pm and 6.30pm sittings, after which it's walk-ins only (Tuesday and Sunday are the easiest nights to score a table). (☑07-3160 3123; www.longtime.com.au; 610 Ann St; mains $15-45; ⊙5.30-10pm Tue-Thu & Sun, to 10.30pm Fri & Sat; ☎; ☒Fortitude Valley)

Les Bubbles

STEAK $$

9 Map p68, A3

From the red-neon declaration – 'Quality meat has been served here since 1982' – to the photos of crooks and cops, this sassy steakhouse relishes its former brothel days. Today the only thing on the menu is superb steak frites, served with unlimited fries and salad. Simply choose your sauce (try the green peppercorn and cognac option) and your libation. (☑07-3251 6500; www.lesbubbles.com.au; 144 Wickham St, Fortitude Valley; steak frites $30; ⊙noon-11pm Sun-Thu, to midnight Fri & Sat; ☒Fortitude Valley)

Tinderbox
ITALIAN $$

10 Map p68, D2

Popular with on-point James St peeps, this modern, mosaic-clad bistro straddles a leafy laneway by the Palace Centro cinemas. The menu is a share-friendly, Italian affair, spanning spicy 'nduja (spreadable pork salumi) arancini and seared cuttlefish with chilli and rocket, to perfectly charred wood-fired pizzas including the stand-out *funghi* (porcini mushrooms, mozzarella and roasted onion). Wash it all down with an innovative cocktail. (☎07-3852 3744; www.thetinderbox.com.au; 7/31 James St, Fortitude Valley; pizzas $20-24, mains $28; ☻5pm-late Tue-Sun; ☒470, ☒Fortitude Valley)

E'cco
MODERN AUSTRALIAN $$$

11 Map p68, A4

Years on, E'cco remains one of the state's gastronomic highlights. Polished yet personable staff deliver beautifully balanced, visually arresting dishes, which might see cured ocean trout flavoured with oyster emulsion or perfect suckling pig meet its match in smoked carrot purée, kimchi and spicy 'nduja. The kitchen offers a smaller, dedicated vegetarian menu (mains $30 to $38) as well as a highly recommended, good-value tasting menu for the full effect. (☎07-3831 8344; www.eccobistro.com.au; 100 Boundary St; mains $36-42, 5-course tasting menu $89; ☻noon-2.30pm Tue-Fri, 6pm-late Tue-Sat; ☒; ☒174, 230, 300)

SUZANNE LONG/AMY STOCK PHOTO ©

Cloudland (p74)

Madame Rouge

FRENCH $$$

12 Map p68, D2

Dark and sexy, Madame Rouge sets a very Parisian scene with red-velvet curtains, tasselled table lamps and Toulouse-Lautrec prints. The menu – co-designed by powerhouse chef Philip Johnson of E'cco fame – reads like a greatest hits of French gastronomy: gratinated goats-cheese souffle; slow-cooked duck leg with puy lentils and black cabbage; and crème brûlée. A beautiful, skilful ode to classic Gallic decadence. (☏07-3252 8881; www.madamerougebistro.com.au; 100 McLachlan St, Fortitude Valley; mains $30-36; ⏰5pm-midnight Tue-Thu & Sat, noon-midnight Fri, noon-5pm Sun; 🚉Fortitude Valley)

Drinking

Gerard's Bar

WINE BAR

13 Map p68, D2

A stylish, grown-up bar that's one of Brisbane's best. Perch yourself at the polished concrete bar, chose an unexpected drop from the sharply curated wine list, and couple with standout bar snacks that include flawless croquettes and prized Jamón Iberico de Belotta. If you're craving a cocktail, try the signature 'Gerard the Drunk', an intriguing, climate-appropriate medley of vodka, passionfruit, pomegranate and rose water. (☏07-3252 2606; www.gerardsbar.com.au; 13a/23 James St; ⏰3-10pm Mon-Thu, noon-late Fri & Sat; 🚌470, 🚉Fortitude Valley)

APO

COCKTAIL BAR

14 Map p68, D4

A smart, quality-driven establishment, the APO was once an apothecary (hence the name). It's a dark, moody, two-level space, where Victorian brickwork contrasts with polished concrete floors and the odd marble feature wall. Drinks are sharp, sophisticated and include bottled single-batch cocktails such as a rhubarb-and-vanilla negroni. Topping it off is a smashing menu of French-Lebanese-inspired bites, including a not-to-be-missed Lebanese taco. (☏07-3252 2403; www.theapo.com.au; 690 Ann St; ⏰3pm-1am Tue, noon-1am Wed, Thu & Sun, noon-3am Fri & Sat; 🚉Fortitude Valley)

Eleven

ROOFTOP BAR

15 Map p68, C2

Slip into your slinkiest threads for Brisbane's finest rooftop retreat, its marble bar pouring a competent list of libations, including pickled-onion-pimped martinis and high-flying French champagnes. Drink in the multi-million-dollar view, which takes in the city skyline and Mt Coot-tha beyond, and schmooze to DJ-spun tunes later in the week. The dress code is especially strict on Friday and Saturday evenings; see the website. (☏07-3067 7447; www.elevenroof topbar.com.au; 757 Ann St; ⏰noon-midnight Tue-Thu & Sun, to 3am Fri & Sat; 🚉Fortitude Valley)

Cloudland BAR

16 Map p68, B3

Jaws hit the floor at this opulent, multilevel bar, club and Pan-Asian restaurant. Named for a much-loved, long-demolished 1940s Brisbane dance hall, Cloudland has birdcage booths, lush foliage and vast chandeliers that are best described as enchanted forest meets sheikh palace meets Addams Family gothic. Free salsa lessons on Thursday from 9pm. (📞07-3872 6600; www.katarzyna.com.au/venues/cloudland; 641 Ann St; ⏰4pm-late Tue-Thu, 11.30am-late Fri-Sun; 🚈Fortitude Valley)

Family CLUB

17 Map p68, B3

Queue up for one of Brisbane's biggest and mightiest clubs. The music here is phenomenal, pumping through four levels with myriad dance floors, bars, themed booths and elite DJs from home and away. Running on Sunday, the 'Fluffy' dance party is a big hit with Brisbane's younger, hotter, gay party peeps. (📞07-3852 5000; www.thefamily.com.au; 8 McLachlan St; ⏰9pm-3.30am Fri-Sun; 🚈Fortitude Valley)

Holey Moley Golf Club COCKTAIL BAR

18 Map p68, D3

Minigolf, in a church, with cocktails is what awaits at Holey Moley (best booked ahead). Order a Putty Professor (rum, milk, chocolate sauce, peanut butter, Reese's Peanut Butter Cup, crushed Maltesers) and tee off on one of two courses. Each of the 18 holes is themed; the standout *Game of Thrones*–themed Iron Throne is by local artist Cezary Stulgis. Kids welcome until 5pm. (📞1300 727 833; www.holeymoley.com.au; 25 Warner St; 9-hole minigolf game per person $16.50; ⏰noon-late Mon-Fri, 10am-late Sat & Sun; 🚈Fortitude Valley)

Woolly Mammoth Alehouse BAR

19 Map p68, B3

The combination of craft beer, giant Jenga and 4m shuffleboard table is not lost on Millennials, who stream into this big, polished playpen to let the good times roll. Brew types include IPAs, saisons and goses, most of which hail from Australian microbreweries. Check the website to see what's playing on the Mane Stage,

Local Life
At Sixes & Sevens

In an old corner weatherboard, the maze of spaces **At Sixes & Sevens** (Map p68, E2; 📞07-3358 6067; www.sixes.com.au; 67 James St; ⏰11am-midnight; 🚌470, 🚈Fortitude Valley) slinky gastro-bar includes fireplace and armchairs, intimate front porch and Astroturf yard. The latter is especially heaving on Friday and Saturday nights, when the local council of cool descend for craft beers, pitchers of punch and the see-and-be-seen vibe. Bar bites include moreish beef short ribs with spice BBQ and cola marinade.

which could be anything from comedy to UK hip-hop. (📞07-3257 4439; www. woollymammoth.com.au; 633 Ann St; ⏲4pm-late Tue-Thu, from noon Fri-Sun; 🚉Fortitude Valley)

Elixir ROOFTOP BAR

20 📍 Map p68, B3

What rooftop Elixir lacks in views it makes up for in ambience. Hurry up the stairs for a sultry, tropical playpen of lush leaves, flickering tealights, DJ-spun beats and languid day beds. Refresh with craft beers or Elixir's Fresh Market martini, a twist on the classic using hand-picked market fruits. Check the website for weekly drinks and food promotions. (📞07-3363 5599; www.elixirrooftop.com.au; 646 Ann St; ⏲4pm-late Wed-Fri, 1pm-late Sat & Sun; 🚉Fortitude Valley)

Cru Bar & Cellar WINE BAR

21 📍 Map p68, D2

A sassy enoteca with fold-back windows, Cru seduces oenophiles with a ferocious wine list. A hefty number of drops by the glass span all price points, while the wine shop out back stocks an impressive selection, including a robust booty of French wines, blue-blooded Italian amarone, even Queensland tempranillo. The food is a little hit and miss; stick to the oysters and cheese. (📞07-3252 1744; www.crubar. com; 22 James St; ⏲bar 11am-late, wine shop 9am-7pm Sat-Thu, 9am-8pm Fri; 🚌470, 🚉Fortitude Valley)

SUZANNE LONG/ALAMY STOCK PHOTO ©

Winn Lane (p67)

Bowery COCKTAIL BAR

22 📍 Map p68, D4

True to its name, dim-and-skinny Bowery evokes downtown Manhattan with its exposed brickwork, gilded mirrors, booths and foot-worn floorboards. Nurse a well-crafted cocktail while tapping to live jazz on weekdays and scrumptious DJ mashups on weekends. (📞07-3252 0202; www. facebook.com/thebowerybar; 676 Ann St; ⏲5pm-late Tue-Sun; 🚉Fortitude Valley)

DAVID WALL/ALAMY STOCK PHOTO ©

Breakfast Creek Hotel

Breakfast Creek Hotel PUB

23 Map p68, C1

Built in 1889 and sporting an eclectic French-Renaissance style, the Breakfast Creek Hotel is a Brisbane icon. The pub offers various bars and dining areas, including a beer garden and an art-deco 'private bar' where the wooden kegs are spiked daily at noon. A converted electricity substation on-site is now home to Substation No 41, an urbane bar with more than 400 rums in its inventory. (07-3262 5988; www. breakfastcreekhotel.com; 2 Kingsford Smith Dr, Albion; 10am-late; 300, 302, 305)

Wickham Hotel PUB

24 Map p68, B2

The crowd may not be quite as LGBT these days, but this grand old dame continues to draw a chilled, mixed crowd for lazy, easy boozing. Kick back in the beer garden and toast to one of the Valley's most fetching-looking pubs. (07-3852 1301; www. thewickham.com.au; 308 Wickham St; 6.30am-late Mon-Fri, 10am-late Sat & Sun; Fortitude Valley)

Entertainment

Beat MegaClub   CLUB

25 ⭐ Map p68, D4

Five rooms + seven bars + three chill-out areas + hard house/electro/retro/techno/hip-hop beats = the perfect storm for dance junkies. It's big with the gay and lesbian crowd, with regular drag shows and a dedicated bar, the campalicious Cockatoo Club. (www.thebeatmegaclub.com.au; 677 Ann St, Fortitude Valley; ◷8pm-5am Mon-Sat, from 5pm Sun; 🚉Fortitude Valley)

The Zoo   LIVE MUSIC

26 ⭐ Map p68, E4

Going strong since 1992, the Zoo has surrendered a bit of musical territory to Brightside, but it is still a grungy spot for indie rock, folk, acoustic, hip-hop, reggae and electronic acts, with no shortage of raw talent. Recent acts have included Gold Coast garage rockers Bleeding Knees Club and American indie pop artist Toro y Moi. (☎07-3854 1381; www.thezoo.com.au; 711 Ann St, Fortitude Valley; ◷7pm-late Wed-Sun; 🚉Fortitude Valley)

Judith Wright Centre of Contemporary Arts   PERFORMING ARTS

Home to both a medium-sized and intimate performance space, this free-thinking arts incubator hosts an eclectic array of cultural treats, including contemporary dance, circus and visual arts. Housing the Institute of Modern Art (see 1 ◎ Map p68, C3), it's also the hub for the hugely popular **Bigsound Festival** (www.bigsound.org.au; ◷Sep), a three-day music fest. Scan the website for upcoming performances and exhibitions. (☎07-3872 9000; www.judithwrightcentre.com; 420 Brunswick St, Fortitude Valley; ◷box office 11am-4pm Mon-Fri; 🛜; 🚉Fortitude Valley)

Crowbar   LIVE MUSIC

27 ⭐ Map p68, B2

A haven of metal, hard-core and punk: black-clad musos of menace from around Australia, the US, the UK, Europe and Japan, in-yer-face and unrelenting. Check the website for special events (flash tattoo exhibition, anyone?). (www.facebook.com/crowbar brisbane; 243 Brunswick St, Fortitude Valley; ◷5pm-late Wed-Sun; 🚉Fortitude Valley)

Local Life
Cheap Flicks

On see-and-be-seen James St, **Palace Centro** (Map p68, D2; ☎07-3852 4488; www.palacecinemas.com.au; 39 James St, Fortitude Valley; adult/child $18/12; ◷9am-late; 🚌470, 🚉Fortitude Valley) screens quality mainstream releases as well as independent films. It also hosts a French film festival in March/April. Discounted $9 tickets are offered on Monday.

Brightside

LIVE MUSIC

28 ⭐ Map p68, D3

The foundation stone of this 1906 church says 'To the glory of God'. But it's the god of live alternative rock the faithful are here to worship these days: heavy, impassioned, unhinged and unfailingly loud. Acts usually hit the stage Thursday to Saturday, playing anything from punk, hardcore and metal to indie, alternative and pop. Just like 1991, minus the cigarettes. (www.thebrightsidebrisbane.com.au; 27 Warner St, Fortitude Valley; ⊗noon-late Tue-Fri, 5pm-5am Sat; 🛜; 🚉Fortitude Valley)

Shopping

Camilla

FASHION & ACCESSORIES

29 🔒 Map p68, D2

Fans of Camilla's statement-making silk kaftans include Beyoncé and Oprah Winfrey. And while the label may be Bondi based, its wildly patterned, resort-style creations – which also include frocks, tops, jumpsuits and swimwear – are just the ticket for languid lounging in chichi Brisbane restaurants and bars. Fierce and fabulous, these pieces aren't cheap, with kaftans starting from $500 and bikinis at around $300. (📞07-3852 6030; www.camilla.com.au; 1/19 James St; ⊗9.30am-5pm Mon-Wed, Fri & Sat, to 7pm Thu, 10am-4pm Sun; 🚌470, 🚉Fortitude Valley)

Fallow

FASHION & ACCESSORIES

30 🔒 Map p68, D4

Up a flight of stairs is this brooding chamber of avant-garde men's fashion. The focus is on sculptural, androgynous pieces from cult-status ateliers not usually stocked in Australia (think Germany's Pal Offner and Denmark's Aleksandr Manamis). Accessories include handmade fragrances from France's Mad et Len and an exquisite collection of handmade jewellery, including Gothic- and Edwardian-inspired pieces by Brisbane-based Luke Maninov. (📞07-3854 0155; www.fallow.com.au; Level 1, 354 Brunswick St; ⊗11am-5pm Mon-Fri, 10am-5pm Sat, 11am-4pm Sun; 🚉Fortitude Valley)

RICHARD I'ANSON/GETTY IMAGES ©

Butter Beats

Tym Guitars

MUSIC

31 Map p68, E4

Cult-status music store Tym stocks everything from vintage guitars and amps to handmade guitar pedals. (It's the kind of place where you might find a limited-edition pedal made by the likes of American alt-rocker J Mascis of Dinosaur Jr.) Tym's vinyl selection includes an especially notable collection of punk, stoner and psychedelic rock records, and the space hosts monthly alt-rock gigs. (☏07-3161 5863; www.tymguitars.com.au; 5 Winn St; ⏰10am-5pm Tue-Thu & Sat, to 7pm Fri, 11am-4pm Sat; ☒Fortitude Valley)

Butter Beats

MUSIC

32 Map p68, B3

Rare and collectable records in the Valley, including old-school Aussie indie. If they don't have it, they'll find it for you. (☏07-3257 3257; www.butterbeatsrecordstore.com; 11/8 Duncan St; ⏰11am-5pm; ☒Fortitude Valley)

Explore

New Farm

New Farm is Fortitude Valley's comfortable neighbour, a verdant corner of graceful Queenslander homes, moderne apartment blocks and lush subtropical gardens. Tranquil streets harbour snug local cafes and eateries, and the suburb's namesake park is home to one of Brisbane's best cultural centres and farmers markets. Nearby Newstead boasts a growing booty of microbreweries and cafes.

The Sights in a Day

 If it's Saturday, head in early to browse the weekly **Jan Powers Farmers Market** (p83; pictured left). If not, start the day with a walk along the park's riverfront to the **Brisbane Powerhouse** (p82), an industrial behemoth turned arts centre.

Around lunch, step inside for old-meets-new interiors, rotating exhibitions and coffee at **Watt** (p90) or **Bar Alto** (p91). Continue north along the river on the beautiful 2km New Farm–Newstead Bike Path, from where you'll need to walk 750m north up Skyring Tce to rejoin the riverfront at Waterfront Park. Continue along Skyring Tce to Gasworks Plaza, a former industrial site turned upscale residential and shopping precinct. Just to the south is hip **Newstead Brewing Co** (p92). Further south browse Commercial Rd Antiques.

A few hops northeast of it is Newstead's other famous brewery, **Green Beacon Brewing Co** (p91). Two blocks west of Newstead Brewing Co, however, you will find **The Triffid** (p91), your rocking night stop.

For a local's day in New Farm, see p84.

Top Sights
Brisbane Powerhouse (p82)

Local Life
New Farm Walk (p84)

♥ Best of Brisbane & the Gold Coast

Eating
New Farm Confectionery (p88)

Watt (p90)

Balfour Kitchen (p89)

Drinking & Entertainment
The Triffid (p91)

Green Beacon Brewing Co (p91)

Moonlight Cinema (p92)

Shopping
Jan Powers Farmers Market (p83)

Commercial Road Antiques (p93)

Gasworks Plaza (p93)

Getting There

⛴ **Ferry** CityCat stops at Sydney St at the southern end of New Farm and at New Farm Park.

🚌 **Bus** Rte 199 connects New Farm to Fortitude Valley, the city, South Bank and West End. Rtes 300, 306 and 322 run from Newstead to Fortitude Valley, the city and South Bank.

Top Sights
Brisbane Powerhouse

What was once a derelict power station is now the Brisbane Powerhouse, an electrifying hub of culture, creativity and crowds. Here, brooding industrial spaces form a dramatic backdrop for innovative art exhibitions, theatre and dance, live music and comedy. Add river views and a couple of bustling eateries and you have one of the city's most spirit-lifting experiences.

Map p86, D4

box office 07-3358 8600, reception 07-3358 8622

www.brisbanepower house.org

119 Lamington St, New Farm

9am-9pm Tue-Sun

195, 196, New Farm Park

Performances

The main reason to hit the Brisbane Powerhouse is for its year-round feast of cultural offerings. In any given month you can expect an eclectic line-up of both local and international acts, delivering everything from stand-up comedy, bawdy cabaret and modern dance, to provocative theatre, Broadway musical revivals and edgy circus arts that evoke Berlin. The Powerhouse is a hub for a string of annual Brisbane festivals, including the **Brisbane Comedy Festival** (www.briscomfest.com; ⊘Feb/Mar), the **Queensland Cabaret Festival** (www.queensland cabaretfestival.com.au; ⊘Jun) and the LGBT-focused **Melt** (www.brisbanepowerhouse.org/festivals; ⊘Jan/Feb).

Industrial Architecture

Designed by architect Roy Rusden Ogg and constructed in stages between 1928 and 1940, the powerhouse supplied electricity for Brisbane's since-defunct tram system, at the time the largest tram network in the southern hemisphere. Officially decommissioned in 1971, the building became a industrial deco relic before its transformation into the dynamic arts hub you see today. Heading the redevelopment was architect Peter Roy, who ensured that the building's history remained a prominent feature of the redevelopment.

Farmers Market

On Saturday morning the Powerhouse serves as a dramatic backdrop for the gut-rumbling **Jan Powers Farmers Market** (www.janpowersfarmers markets.com.au; ⊘6am-noon Sat). This is one of the city's best-loved weekly farmers markets, luring locals from across town. Sail in on a CityCat catamaran and scan the market stalls for a feast of artisanal edibles, from Brisbane-made bûchette de Chèvre cheese and fragrant loaves of Frankenlaib bread, to salted-caramel lamingtons.

☑ **Top Tips**

▶ Free events run throughout the year, including art exhibitions, thought-provoking talks and a weekly 'Powerkids' creative play session for kids up to five and their guardians. The latter is hosted by artists, who engage their young participants in a variety of artistic activities, from dance and theatre to digital and visual art. See the Powerhouse website for all upcoming free activities.

✗ **Take a Break**

Kick back with interesting Italian wines and Italian-inspired bistro dishes on the balcony at Bar Alto (p91). Downstairs, vibrant see-and-be-seen Watt (p90) is an equally buzzing, contemporary option.

Local Life
New Farm Walk

Comfortable, old New Farm is Brisbane at its sultry best. Delicate wooden abodes flank sleepy, bougainvillea-dotted streets and cool little cafes serve up beautiful local produce. This is a place for relaxing waterside walks and architectural exploration. Come the weekend, it's also the place for bustling market trawls and long, lazy afternoons kicking back with drinks and tunes by the river.

❶ Chouquette

Start on a sweet note at **Chouquette** (☎07-3358 6336; www.chouquette.com.au; 19 Barker St; items $2.50-11; ⏱6.30am-4pm Wed-Sat, to 12.30pm Sun; 🍴; 🚌195, 196, 199), one of the city's top pastisseries. If you're lucky, you'll score a table on the pavement, the best spot to people watch over flaky French pastries and velvety café au lait. This is a much-loved morning hang-out for locals, especially on Saturday and Sunday

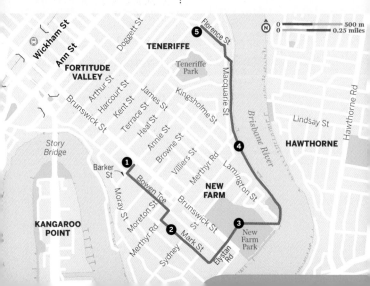

mornings, when couples head across armed with sunglasses and the paper.

2 Mark St

New Farm claims some of Brisbane's most beautiful heritage houses and you'll find an eclectic mix along Mark St. Stroll the two blocks for a feast of vernacular architectural details, from wraparound verandahs with flouncy cast-iron or timber balustrades, to latticed timber screens, louvres and decorative window hoods. Providing contrast in the background are the tops of Brisbane skyscrapers.

3 New Farm Park

New Farm Park (www.newfarmpark. com.au; Brunswick St; ⏱24hr; 🚌195, 196, 🚢New Farm Park) is a collective backyard for the locals, here to walk their pugs, heed the commands of their personal trainers or simply set the kids free among the Moreton Bay fig trees. On Saturday morning you'll find them stocking up on mangoes, cheeses and other regional edibles at the ever-popular Jan Powers Farmers Market.

4 Brisbane Riverwalk

On any given morning or afternoon, you'll find Fitbit-wired locals jogging or cycling the **pedestrian promenade** (🚌195, 196, 🚢Sydney St) that runs from the Brisbane Powerhouse to Teneriffe further north. It's a gorgeous stretch, flanked by the river on one side and coveted real-estate on the other. Look out for the heritage-listed CSR Refinery, a late-19th-century sugar refinery turned apartment complex.

5 Sourced Grocer

On a Tenriffe side street, laid-back **Sourced Grocer** (📞07-3852 6734; www.sourcedgrocer.com.au; 11 Florence St, Teneriffe; dishes $7-23; ⏱7am-3pm Mon-Sat, 8am-3pm Sun, shop 7am-8pm Mon-Thu, to 7pm Fri, to 5pm Sat, to 4pm Sun; 🚌199, 393, 🚢Teneriffe) will have you perched on a cushioned milk crate, sipping a decent coffee and noshing on beautifully presented dishes. The food here preferences quality, regional ingredients, a philosophy that extends to the goods on the shelves. Scan them for unusual local treats that might include soda syrups with flavours including Thai basil and galangal.

A

B

C

D

Skyring Tce

18 NEWSTEAD

Longland St

Stratton St

11

Doggett St

13

Wyandra St

Helen St

12

Commercial Rd

Teneriffe

Fireworks
Gallery

1

Commercial Rd

17

Florence St

Commercial Rd

Macquarie St

7

Wickham St

Ann St

TENERIFFE

0   500 m
0   0.25 miles

McLachlan St

Robertson St

Doggett St

Terrace St

Suzanne
O'Connell
Gallery

Arthur St

3

Harcourt St

James St

Teneriffe
Park

Kingsholme St

Merthyr Rd

New Farm to Newstead Trail

Lindsay St

HAWTHORN

Edwina
Corlette
Gallery

2

Kent St

Terrace St

Heal St

Brunswick St

9

8

Annie St

Browne St

NEW FARM

Villiers St

Merthyr Rd

5

Lamington St

14

Hawthorne

Story
Bridge

Bowen Tce

15

Barker

16

4

Moray St

Moreton St

Merthyr Rd

Sydney St

Bowen Tce

Brunswick St

New
Farm
Park

**Brisbane
Powerhouse**

10

Brisbane Riverwalk

CityCat Ferry

CityHopper Ferry

KANGAROO
POINT

Dockside

Cairns St

Sydney
St

6

Oxlade Dr

Merthyr
Park

New Farm
Park

CityCat Ferry

Brisbane River

Norman
Park

Shafston Ave

Wynnum Rd

RICHARD I'ANSON/GETTY IMAGES ©

Fireworks Gallery

Sights

Fireworks Gallery
GALLERY

1 ◎ Map p86, B1

What looks like a garage is in fact one of Brisbane's best-loved commercial galleries. The space showcases mainly painting and sculpture from emerging and established Australian artists, both Indigenous and non-Indigenous. Group shows are common. (☏ 07-3216 1250; www.fireworks gallery.com.au; 52a Doggett St, Newstead; ☺ 10am-6pm Tue-Fri, to 4pm Sat; ☒ 300, 302, 305, 306, 322, 393, 470)

Edwina Corlette Gallery
GALLERY

2 ◎ Map p86, A3

This refreshing gallery is well known for showcasing intriguing work by both emerging and mid-career artists from Australia and the Asia Pacific region. Both solo and group exhibitions are run, spanning a range of media, from painting, printmaking and sculpture, to photography, digital art and installations. (☏ 07-3358 6555; www.edwinacorlette.com; 2/555 Brunswick St, New Farm; ☺ 10am-5pm Tue-Sat; ☒ 195, 196, 199)

Q Local Life
Brisbane Riverwalk

Jutting out over the city's big, brown waterway, the **Brisbane Riverwalk** (Map p86, A4; ⚑ Sydney St; ⛴195, 196) offers a novel way of surveying the Brisbane skyline. The 870m-long path – divided into separate walking and cycling lanes – runs between New Farm and the Howard St Wharves, from where you can continue towards central Brisbane itself. The Riverwalk replaces the original floating walkway, sadly washed away in the floods of 2011.

Suzanne O'Connell Gallery
GALLERY

3 ◉ Map p86, B2

Set in a traditional Queenslander, this private gallery showcases high-quality Indigenous art from across the continent. Works range from painting and sculpture, to ceramics, works on bark and fibre objects. Check the website for exhibition openings. (☏07-3358 5811; www.suzanneoconnell.com; 93 James St, New Farm; admission free; ⏱11am-4pm Wed-Sat; ⛴470)

Eating

New Farm Confectionery
SWEETS $

4 ✖ Map p86, B3

For a locavore sugar rush, squeeze into this tiny confectioner, located on the side of the New Farm Six Cinemas. From the macadamia brittle and chocolate-coated Madagascan vanilla marshmallow, to the slabs of blackberry-infused white chocolate, all of the products are made using natural, top-tier ingredients. Nostalgic types shouldn't miss the sherbet powder, made with actual fruit and paired with lollipops for gleeful dipping. (☏07-3139 0964; www.newfarmconfectionery.com.au; 14 Barker St, New Farm; sweets from $3; ⏱10am-6pm Wed & Thu, to 9.30pm Fri & Sat; ⛴195, 196, 199)

Little Loco
CAFE $

5 ✖ Map p86, C3

A white space speckled green with plants, this little New Farm local keeps peeps healthy with dishes such as the Green Bowl, a tasty, feel-great combo of kale, spinach, broccolini, feta, pomegranate seeds, avocado and dukkah. There's no shortage of vegetarian and paleo bites, as well as dairy- and gluten-free options. Such salubrious credentials make sense given that the cafe's owner is Brisbane soccer player Daniel Bowles. (☏07-3358 5706; www.facebook.com/littlelococafe; 121 Merthyr Rd, New Farm; breakfast $8-17, lunch $14.50-17; ⏱6am-3pm Mon-Fri, 6.30am-2.30pm Sat & Sun; ✎; ⛴196, 199, 195)

Double Shot
CAFE $

6 ✖ Map p86, B5

With its button-cute wooden porch, manicured hedge and upbeat furniture, petite Double Shot is a hit with brunching mums, dog-walkers and polished, suit-clad realtors. Join the New Farm crew for good coffee, coconut bread with whipped ricotta, Spanish sardines on sourdough or refreshing green papaya, coconut and chicken salad. Tapas served from 3pm on Friday. (☑07-3358 6556; www.facebook.com/doubleshotnewfarm; 125 Oxlade Dr, New Farm; mains $11.50-19.50; ⏰7am-3pm Wed, Thu & Sat, to 9pm Fri, 8am-3pm Sun; 🚍196, 🚢Sydney St)

Wilde Kitchen HEALTH FOOD $

Chow guilt-free at this lean, low-key cafe, where everything on the menu is paleo, vegetarian, gluten-free or dairy-free. Kickstart the AM with warm coconut and kaffir lime rice, or lunch on the especially popular sticky pork. Wholesome snacks include date truffles and Jaffa slices, best paired with a spicy, caffeine-free 'golden latte' (made with turmeric, cinnamon, honey, coconut oil, pepper and saffron). (☑07-3252 2595; www.wildekitchen.com.au; cnr Macqaurie & Florence Sts, Teneriffe; dishes $9.50-19.50; ⏰6.30am-2.30pm; 🛜🖌; 🚍199, 🚢Teneriffe)

Balfour Kitchen MODERN AUSTRALIAN $$

8 🍴 Map p86, A3

Should you nosh in the dining room, on the verandah or among the frangipani in the courtyard? This polished cafe-restaurant creates a very Queensland conundrum. Wherever you may land

---

Understand
Unreal Real Estate

When the GFC bit hard in 2008, economists and bankers across the Western world very sensibly said, 'Whoops! We've been lending people money they can't afford to pay back, and they've been blowing it on home loans that are too expensive' – and real estate prices tumbled. But not in Australia. There was a mining boom in full swing: nobody worried about ridiculous housing prices when there was always another chunk of Queensland or Western Australia waiting to be exhumed and sold to China. Australians just kept on buying pricey houses, driving the market skywards.

Now – with the mining boom over and society having reached a tipping point where the median house price is more than five times the median annual household income – Australian real estate prices are among the least affordable on the planet. Buying a house in Brisbane is now all but unattainable for young first-home buyers.

Fears of a property 'bubble' about to burst are rife, but as long as interest rates remain low and the perception that Australia is the 'lucky country' and somehow immune to global strife endures, Queensland's real estate addiction will be hard to break.

a linen-covered table, swoon over nuanced, sophisticated dishes, from morning brioche French toast with hazelnut, chocolate ganache and sour cherries, to evening hot-smoked barramundi paired with charred cauliflower and pil-pil sauce. Live tunes accompany Sunday lunch. (📞1300 597 540; www.spicersretreats.com/spicers-balfour-hotel/dining; Spicers Balfour Hotel, 37 Balfour St, New Farm; breakfast $14-25, dinner mains $32-38; ⏱6.30-11am, noon-2.30pm & 5.30-8.30pm Mon-Fri, from 7.30am Sat & Sun; 🚌195, 196, 199)

Himalayan Cafe
NEPALI **$$**

 9 🍴 Map p86, B3

Awash with prayer flags, this free-spirited, karma-positive restaurant pulls in the punters with authentic Tibetan and Nepalese dishes such as tender *fhaiya deakau* (lamb with veggies, coconut milk, sour cream and spices). Repeat the house mantra: 'May positive forces be with every single living thing that exists'. (📞07-3358 4015; 640 Brunswick St, New Farm; mains $16-27; ⏱5.30-9.30pm Tue-Thu & Sun, to 10.30pm Fri & Sat; 🍴; 🚌195, 196, 199)

Watt
MODERN AUSTRALIAN **$$**

 10 🍴 Map p86, D4

On the riverbank level of the Brisbane Powerhouse is Watt, a breezy, contemporary space made for long, lazy vino sessions and people watching. Keep it casual with bar bites like Cuban fish tacos and manchego croquettes, or book a table in the restaurant for

New Farm Park (p85)

farm-to-table options such as wild Bendigo rabbit pappardelle with smoked speck, hazelnut, watercress pesto and parmesan. (☎07-3358 5464; www.wattbrisbane.com.au; Brisbane Powerhouse, 119 Lamington St, New Farm; bar food $10-29, restaurant $25-34; ⏰10.30am-6pm Mon, to 10pm Tue-Fri, 8am-10pm Sat & Sun; 🚌195, 196, 🚢New Farm Park)

Bar Alto
ITALIAN $$$

At the arts-pumping Brisbane Powerhouse, in the same building as Watt (see 10 ❌ Map p86, D4), this snappy upstairs bar-restaurant draws culture vultures and general bon vivants with its enormous balcony, at the ready with gorgeous river view. Local ingredients sing in Italian-inspired dishes, such as spanner-crab gnocchi, while the solid wine list includes a good number of interesting Italian drops. Book ahead if dining Friday to Sunday (Sunday lunch can book out weeks in advance in summer). (☎07-3358 1063; www.baralto.com.au; Brisbane Powerhouse, 119 Lamington St, New Farm; mains $27-33; ⏰restaurant 11.30am-9pm Tue-Thu & Sun, to 10pm Fri & Sat, bar 9.30am-late Tue-Sun; 🚌195, 196, 🚢New Farm Park)

Drinking

The Triffid
BAR

11 🚇 Map p86, B1

Not only does the Triffid have an awesome beer garden (complete with shipping-container bars and a

Top Tip

All-night Espresso

New Farm is home to Brisbane's only 24-hour espresso bar, **Death Before Decaf** (3/760 Brunswick St; ⏰24hr; 🚌195, 196, 199). Day or night, the place pours some of the best brew in town. Good news for insomniacs or those seeking sobriety after a night on the tiles in neighbouring Newstead or Fortitude Valley.

cassette-themed mural honouring Brisbane bands), it's also one of the city's top live-music venues. Music acts span local, Aussie and international talent, playing in a barrel-vaulted WWII hangar with killer acoustics. It's hardly surprising given that the place is owned by former Powderfinger bassist John Collins. (☎07-3171 3001; www.thetriffid.com.au; 7-9 Stratton St, Newstead; 🚌300, 302, 305, 306, 322, 393)

Green Beacon Brewing Co
MICROBREWERY

12 🚇 Map p86, B1

In a cavernous warehouse in post-industrial Teneriffe, Green Beacon brews some of Brisbane's best beers. The liquid beauties ferment in vast stainless-steel vats behind the long bar before flowing through the taps and onto your grateful palate. Choose from six core beers or seasonal specials such as blood-orange IPA.

Peckish? Decent bites include fresh local seafood, and there's always a guest food truck parked out front. (☏07-3252 8393; www.greenbeacon.com.au; 26 Helen St, Teneriffe; ☺noon-late; 🛜; 🚌393, 470, ⛴Teneriffe)

Newstead Brewing Co

MICROBREWERY

13 Map p86, B1

What was once a bus depot is now a pumping microbrewery, its 12 taps pouring six standard house brews, one cider and five seasonal beers (dubbed the 'fun stuff' by one staffer). For an enlightening overview, order the paddle board of four different brews. If beer doesn't rock your boat, knock back cocktails, craft spirits or wine from a small, engaging list of smaller producers. (☏07-3172 2488; www.newstead brewing.com.au; 85 Doggett St, Newstead; ☺11am-midnight; 🚌60, 393, 470, ⛴Teneriffe)

Bitter Suite

BAR

14 🍺 Map p86, C3

Hiding out on a quiet New Farm backstreet is this lofty red-brick warehouse, reborn as an effervescent beer barn. Guzzle from more than 60 craft brews, a daily selection of which flows through the taps. Super made-from-scratch bar food too (Peking-duck pancakes) and weekend breakfasts (lemonade scones, anyone?). (☏07-3254 4426; www.bittersuite.com.au; 2/75 Welsby St; ☺11.30am-10.30pm Tue-Thu, to 11.30pm Fri, 8am-11.30pm Sat, 8am-10pm Sun; 🚌196, 199)

Gertie's Bar & Lounge

WINE BAR

15 🍺 Map p86, B3

Gertie's always seems to have local peeps sipping wine and cocktails inside the fold-back windows. It's a moody, deliciously old-school spot, with old soul on the stereo, retro photos on the walls and checkered floors. Great for martinis and people watching, though not nearly as fabulous on the food front. (699 Brunswick St, New Farm; ☺5pm-midnight Tue & Wed, from 4pm Thu-Sat, 4-11pm Sun; 🚌195, 196, 199)

Entertainment

New Farm Six Cinemas

CINEMA

16 ⭐ Map p86, B3

When those subtropical heavens open up, take refuge at New Farm's historic movie palace. Recently remodelled and restored, its six, state-of-the-art screening rooms show mostly mainstream new releases. Tuesday is popular with penny-pinching film buffs, with all tickets a bargain $8. (☏07-3358 4444; www.newfarmcinemas. com.au; 701 Brunswick St, New Farm; adult/child $16/10; ☺10am-late; 🚌195, 196, 199)

Moonlight Cinema

CINEMA

From early December through to early March, New Farm Park becomes an outdoor cinema, with nightly films screened Wednesday to Sunday beside the Brisbane Powerhouse arts centre (p82). Films include current mainstream releases as well as the odd cult

Brisbane Riverwalk (p88)

classic. Arrive early to get a spot. (www.moonlight.com.au; Brisbane Power-house, 119 Lamington Rd, New Farm; adult/child $17/12.50; ⊙7pm Wed-Sun; 🚌195, 196, 🚢New Farm Park)

Shopping

Commercial Road Antiques

ANTIQUES

17 🅰 Map p86, B1

Whether you're on the prowl for a Victorian dresser, a mid-century armchair or a '60s beatnik frock, chances are you'll find it in this warren of eclectic antiques and retro. It's especially great for vintage glassware, and there's usually a good selection of tribal and Asian decorative objects. (☎07-3852 2352; 85 Commercial Rd, Teneriffe; ⊙10am-5pm; 🚌393, 470, 🚢Teneriffe)

Gasworks Plaza

SHOPPING CENTRE

18 🅰 Map p86, B1

A small, polished, indoor-outdoor shopping complex with cafes, bars and mostly speciality food stores at the redeveloped gasworks in Newstead. Retailers include major supermarket chain Woolworths. (www.gasworksplaza.com.au; 76 Skyring Tce, Newstead; ⊙supermarket 7am-9pm, other shops vary; 🚌60, 300, 302, 305, 306, 322, 393, 🚢Teneriffe)

Explore

Kangaroo Point & Woolloongabba

Kangaroo Point spreads across a sinuous peninsula east of the city centre. Its imposing Story Bridge and vertiginous western cliffs offer blockbuster views of the Brisbane skyline. You can scale both the bridge and cliffs, while the riverbank below lures with its waterside pathway. Woolloongabba is an oft-overlooked inner suburb where heritage facades and antique stores make for a charming interlude.

The Sights in a Day

☀ You could easily while away a morning or afternoon in Woolloongabba, brunching or lunching at one of the cafes or bistros on Logan Rd before popping into a gallery or two, snapping the street art on Trafalgar St and treasure hunting at the Woolloongabba Antique Centre.

☼ In the afternoon, stop for coffee at the **Cliffs Cafe** (p99) in Kangaroo Point to soak up the view, then head down the steps to the bottom of the cliffs to kick back by the river with a book or to hire a bike or kayak. If you're after a serious thrill, book a **Story Bridge Adventure Climb** (p97; pictured left), especially spectacular at twilight.

☾ After dark, hit the **Story Bridge Hotel** (p101) for beers in the garden, or retreat to the nearby **Brisbane Jazz Club** (p101) for romantic skyline views and smooth, sultry tunes.

💚 **Best of Brisbane & the Gold Coast**

Activities
Story Bridge Adventure Climb (p97)

Riverlife (p97)

Eating
1889 Enoteca (p99)

Pearl Cafe (p99)

Sorellina (p99)

Drinking & Entertainment
Canvas Club (p100)

Story Bridge Hotel (p101)

Brisbane Jazz Club (p101)

Getting There

🚌 **Bus** Rte 234 crosses Kangaroo Point. Northbound buses stop at Wickham Tce in Fortitude Valley before continuing to the city. Southbound buses terminate at Woolloongabba Bus Station. From Woolloongabba Bus Station, numerous routes run directly to South Bank and the city.

⛴ **Ferry** The free CityHopper ferry service stops at all three Kangaroo Point terminals. The Kangaroo Point Cross River Ferry connects both Holman St and Thornton St terminals to Eagle St Pier in the city.

Story Bridge

Central
Ann St
Adelaide St
Post Office Square
Queen St

Holman St
CT White Park
Holman St
13

Riverside
Story Bridge Adventure Climb 2
Wharf St

Eagle St Pier
12
Rotherham St

Elizabeth St
Edward St

CITY

Albert St
Alice St

Thornton St

Brisbane River
CityCat Ferry

CityHopperferry

Brisbane River

NEW FARM

Sydney St

Cairns St
KANGAROO POINT

Dockside

City Botanic Gardens

CityHopper Ferry

1
Riverlife

6

Sydney St
Oxlade Dr
Merthyr Park

Mowbray Park
CityCat Ferry

Pacific Mwy

River Tce

Pearson St

Shafston Ave

Mowbray Park
Lytton Rd

Captain Cook Bridge

Maritime Museum

Kangaroo Point Cliffs

Main St

Bell St
Sinclair St

Llewellyn St
Walmsley St
Lockerbie St

Baines St

Wellington Rd

Latrobe St

EAST BRISBANE

Mowbray Tce

Vulture St

Toohey St
Princess St

Elfin St

Vulture St

Stanley St
9
11
Jurgens St
Logan Rd
7
5
8
0   50 m

Pacific Mwy

Main St

WOOLLOONGABBA

See Enlargement

14

10

3
Guido Van Helten Mural

Lisburn St

15
Milani
4

Stanley St

N
0   500 m
0   0.25 miles

For reviews see
◉ Sights   p97
⊗ Eating   p98
▢ Drinking   p100
✪ Entertainment   p101
🔒 Shopping   p101

Kangaroo Point Cliffs (p101)

Sights

Riverlife ADVENTURE SPORTS

1 ⊙ Map p96, B3

Based at the bottom of the Kangaroo Point Cliffs, Riverlife offers numerous active city thrills. Rock climb (from $55), abseil ($45) or opt for a kayak river trip (from $45). The latter includes a booze-and-food 'Paddle and Prawns' option ($85) on Friday and Saturday nights. Also rents out bikes, kayaks and in-line skates. (☏07-3891 5766; www.riverlife.com.au; Naval Stores, Kangaroo Point Bikeway, Kangaroo Point; bikes/in-line skates hire per 4hr $35/40, kayaks per 2hr $35; ⏱9am-5pm; ⛴Thornton St)

Story Bridge Adventure Climb ADVENTURE SPORTS

2 ⊙ Map p96, B1

Scaling Brisbane's most famous bridge is nothing short of thrilling, with unbeatable views of the city – morning, twilight or night. The two-hour climb scales the southern half of the structure, taking you 80m above the twisting, muddy Brisbane River below. Dawn climbs are run on the last Saturday of the month. Minimum age 10 years. (☏1300 254 627; www.sbac.net.au; 170 Main St, Kangaroo Point; climb from $100; ☒234, ⛴Thornton St, Holman St)

Guido Van Helten Mural

PUBLIC ART

3 ◉ Map p96, C5

Dominating a car park on Trafalgar St is this giant monochromatic mural by Brisbane street artist Guido Van Helten. One of Australia's most globally successful street artists, Van Helten created the piece for the 2016 Brisbane Street Art Festival. (Trafalgar St, Woolloongabba)

Milani

GALLERY

4 ◉ Map p96, C5

A well-regarded commercial gallery with cutting-edge Aboriginal and sometimes confronting contemporary artwork. It's in an industrial area surrounded by car yards and hairdressing equipment suppliers – if it looks closed, just turn the door handle.

(☎ 07-3391 0455; www.milanigallery.com.au; 54 Logan Rd, Woolloongabba; admission free; ⏱ 11am-6pm Tue-Sat; ☒ 174, 175, 204)

Eating

Baker's Arms

BAKERY $

5 ✖ Map p96, A5

Wrapped up in London-themed wallpaper and hessian coffee bags, this industrious Woolloongabba bakery turns out freshly baked cakes and tarts, as well as cafe-standard egg dishes, burgers and interesting salads (think pork and pickled watermelon). The coffee is good and best enjoyed leafing through the Baker's stack of daily newspapers. (☎ 07-3391 6599; www.thebakersarms.com.au; 29 Logan Rd, Woolloongabba; pastries from $3.50, dishes $8-18.50; ⏱ 7am-3pm; ☒ 125, 175, 204, 234)

Understand
This Sporting Life

Queenslanders love sport: watching it, talking about it and playing it. On the 'watching' front, in the annual best-of-three State of Origin rugby league clash between the Queensland 'Maroons' and New South Wales 'Blues', normality has been restored, with Queensland winning in 2015 and 2016. Other than a momentary lapse in 2014 when NSW were victorious, Queensland has won the series every time since 2006.

Down on the Gold Coast, preparations are in full swing for the April 2018 Commonwealth Games. With 6600 athletes and officials representing 70 countries, this will be the largest sporting event held in Australia since the 2000 Sydney Olympics. See www.gc2018.com for updates.

Cliffs Cafe

CAFE $

6 Map p96, B3

Looking straight out at the river, sky-line and City Botanic Gardens, lofty Cliffs offers what is arguably the best view of Brisbane. It's a casual, open-air pavilion, serving big breakfasts, panini, burgers, fish and chips, salads and sweet treats. While the food won't necessarily blow your socks off, the unobstructed, postcard panorama will. Kick back with a coffee or beer and count your blessings. (☏07-3391 7771; www.cliffscafe.com.au; 29 River Tce, Kangaroo Point; dishes $6.50-19.50; ☺7am-5pm; ᾒ234)

Pearl Cafe

CAFE $$

7 Map p96, A5

Channelling Melbourne and Paris with its Euro flair, Pearl is one of Brisbane's best-loved weekend brunch spots. There are freshly baked cakes on the counter, a sophisticated selection of spirits on the shelf, and beautiful cafe dishes on the menu. Snub the underwhelming avocado on toast for more inspiring options, among them the popular daytime pork cotoletta. Sandwiches are chunky and generously filled. (☏07-3392 3300; www.facebook.com/pearl.cafe.brisbane; 28 Logan Rd, Woolloongabba; mains $16-34; ☺7am-8pm Tue-Sat, to 3pm Sat & Sun; ᾒ125, 175, 204, 234)

Sorellina

PIZZA $$

8 Map p96, A5

'Little Sister' offers the pizzeria 2.0 experience: chianti bottles are ditched for organic and biodynamic wines, and Napoli posters for Bowie portraits. Good traditions, however, are not thrown out: Sorellina's light, fluffy, Neapolitan-style pizzas are made using quality Italian 00 flour, cold risen for 36 hours before being wood-fired to *perfezione*. Try the chilli-spiked Tuscan kale pizza, best washed down with a Napoli Fizz. (☏07-3391 8459; www.sorellinapizzeria.com; 31 Logan Rd, Woolloongabba; pizzas $20-24; ☺5pm-late Tue-Sun & noon-2.30pm Fri-Sun; ᾒ125, 175, 204, 234)

1889 Enoteca

ITALIAN $$$

9 Map p96, A5

Italian purists rightfully adore this moody, sophisticated bistro and wine store, where pasta is *not* served with a spoon (unless requested) and a Roman-centric menu delivers seductive dishes including *carciofi alla Giuda* (Jewish-Roman-style fried artichoke with parsley and lemon mascarpone) and melt-in-your-mouth gnocchi with pork and fennel sausage, parmesan cream and black-truffle tapenade. Superlative wines include drops from lauded, smaller Italian producers. (☏07-3392 4315; www.1889enoteca.com.au; 10-12 Logan Rd, Woolloongabba; pasta $21-42, mains $32-49; ☺noon-2.30pm & 6-10pm Tue-Fri, 6-10pm Sat, noon-2.30pm Sun; ᾒ125, 175, 204, 234)

Catbird Seat Bistro

MODERN AUSTRALIAN $$$

10 ⊗ Map p96, C5

Behind French-lattice windows, Catbird Seat runs an intimate, soulful affair, its bentwood chairs, blackboard specials and petite bar paging a somewhat Parisian air. Join gourmands and hopeless romantics for beautifully cooked dishes that might see wontons go local with a crocodile filling, or gnocchi get fresh with garden peas, ricotta, mint and lemon. Fish is fresh and dependent on what looked best that morning. (☏07-3392 2645; www.catbirdseatbistro.com.au; 2/888 Stanley St East, East Brisbane; mains $28-36; ⊙noon-2.30pm & 5.30-9pm Tue-Fri, 5-9pm Sat; ⊡184, 185, 210, 212, 230, 235)

Drinking

Canvas Club

COCKTAIL BAR

11 ⊙ Map p96, A5

Slap bang on Woolloongabba's main eating, drinking and shopping strip, Canvas sets a hip, arty scene for cheeky cocktail sessions. Debate the symbolism of the street-art mural while downing seasonal libations like the Don Pablo (rum, amaro and apple-and-cinnamon foam) or the silky smooth Bangarang (tequila, watermelon, chilli, coriander, lime and condensed milk). Smashing. (☏07-3891 2111; www.canvasclub.com.au; 16b Logan Rd, Woolloongabba; ⊙noon-midnight Tue-Fri, from 10am Sat & Sun; ⊡125, 175, 204, 234)

The Gabba

PETER HARRISON/GETTY IMAGES ©

Story Bridge Hotel

PUB

12 Map p96, B2

Beneath the bridge at Kangaroo Point, this beautiful 1886 pub and beer garden is perfect for a pint after a long day exploring. Regular live music and a good choice of drinking and eating areas. (📞07-3391 2266; www.storybridge hotel.com.au; 200 Main St, Kangaroo Point; 🕑6.30am-midnight Sun-Thu, to 1.30am Fri & Sat; 🚌234, 🚋Thornton St, Holman St)

Entertainment

Brisbane Jazz Club

JAZZ

13 ⭐ Map p96, B1

Straight out of the bayou, this tiny riverside jazz shack has been Brisbane's jazz beacon since 1972. Anyone who's anyone in the scene plays here when they're in town. (📞07-3391 2006; www.brisbanejazzclub.com.au; 1 Annie St, Kangaroo Point; adult/under 18yr $31/11; 🕑6.30-11pm Thu-Sat, 5.30-10pm Sun; 🚋Holman St)

The Gabba

STADIUM

14 ⭐ Map p96, C5

You can cheer both AFL football and interstate and international cricket at the Gabba in Woolloongabba. If you're new to cricket, try and get along to a Twenty20 match, which sees the game in its most explosive form. The cricket season runs from late September to March; the football from late March to September. (Brisbane Cricket Ground; www. thegabba.com.au; 411 Vulture St, Woolloongabba; 🚌174, 175, 184, 185, 200)

 Top Tip

Cliff Hangers

A spectacular sight at night with its floodlit vertical rock face, the 20m **Kangaroo Point Cliffs** (🚌234, 🚋Thornton St) on the southern banks of the Brisbane River offer outdoor climbing and abseiling during the day. **Pinnacle Sports** (📞07-3368 3335; www.pinnaclesports.com. au; 2hr abseiling from $80, 3hr climbing from $90) has options that include a two-hour sunset abseil, as well as full-day rock-climbing trips to the Glass House Mountains.

Shopping

Woolloongabba Antique Centre

ANTIQUES

15 Map p96, C5

Brisbane's biggest antiques centre is a veritable sea of memories and design inspiration. Scour its 60-plus stalls for original and upcycled furniture (including Danish Modernist pieces), collectable glassware, Americana, not to mention a super-fun booty of retro fashion for rockabillies and individualist fashionistas. There's an in-house '50s-inspired cafe, as well as a pop-up barber shop (usually snipping on the last Sunday of the month). (📞07-3392 1114; www.woolloongabbaantiquecentre.com; 22 Wellington Rd, Woolloongabba; 🕑9am-5pm; 🚌184, 185, 210, 212, 230, 235)

Top Sights
Gold Coast Theme Parks

Getting There

🚌 **Bus** Gold Coast Tourist Shuttle meets flights into Gold Coast Airport and runs to Gold Coast theme parks. Surfside Buslines also runs to the parks.

The gravity-defying roller coasters, water slides, movie characters and Disneyesque fun at the Gold Coast's American-style theme parks are well known to Aussie families who come from far and wide for the experience.

They offer some seriously dizzying action and, although recently beset with a tragic accident (Dreamworld) and a number of malfunctions, still attract huge crowds.

Wet'n'Wild

Dreamworld

Dreamworld (📞07-5588 1111, 1800 073 300; www.dream world.com.au; Dreamworld Pkwy, Coomera; adult/child $65/55; ⏱10am-5pm) touts itself as Australia's 'biggest' theme park. Thrill Rides, Wiggles World and the Dream-Works experience. Other attractions include Tiger Island, and a range of interactive animal encounters.

Sea World

Sea World (www.seaworld.com.au; adult/child $80/70; ⏱9.30am-5pm) continues to attract controversy for its marine shows, where dolphins and sea lions perform tricks for the crowd. The park also displays penguins and polar bears, and has water slides and roller coasters.

Movie World

Movie World (📞07-5573 3999, 13 33 86; www.movie world.com.au; Pacific Hwy, Oxenford; adult/child $79/69; ⏱9.30am-5pm) is all about movie-themed shows, rides and attractions, including the Batwing Spaceshot, Justice League 3D Ride and Scooby-Doo Spooky Coaster. Batman, Austin Powers, Porky Pig et al roam through the crowds.

Wet'n'Wild

The ultimate water slide at **Wet'n'Wild** (📞07-5556 1660, 13 33 86; www.wetnwild.com.au; Pacific Hwy, Oxenford; adult/child $79/69; ⏱10am-5pm) is the Kamikaze, where you plunge down an 11m drop in a two-person tube at 50km/h. Also pitch-black slides, white-water rapids and wave pools.

Whitewater World

Whitewater World (📞1800 073 300, 07-5588 1111; www.dreamworld.com.au/whitewater-world; Dreamworld Pkwy, Coomera; adult/child $65/55; ⏱10am-4pm Mon-Fri, to 5pm Sat & Sun) features the Cave of Waves, Pipeline Plunge and more than 140 wet and watery activities and slides.

☑ Top Tips

Discount tickets are sold in most of the tourist offices on the Gold Coast or can be bought online. The Mega Pass ($110 per person for 14-day entry) grants unlimited entry to Sea World, Warner Bros. Movie World, Wet'n'Wild and Paradise Country. Dreamworld and WhiteWater World have a Summer Season Pass giving unlimited entry (adult/child $99/79).

✗ Take a Break

You're not supposed to take food or drink into the parks, leaving you at the mercy of high-priced food outlets. Consider a trip to nearby Main Beach for lunch at Peter's Fish Market (p108) or the Pier (p109).

Explore

Surfers Paradise & Main Beach

Built for pleasure and utterly dedicated to sun, surf and the body beautiful, this strip of coast is possibly Australia's most iconic holiday destination. The shimmering Surfer's Paradise high-rises can appear like a make-believe city, and its reputation for tackiness is occasionally deserved. But this is far outstripped by a booming, youthful spirit, startling physical beauty, perfect climate and epic surf breaks.

The Sights in a Day

☀ Hit the beach early (in summer the sun is up at 4.30am) for a walk, swim or surf, or view the surf from above in a **hot-air-balloon flight** (p108), ending with a champagne breakfast. Head to **Bumbles Cafe** (p110) in Surfers Paradise for a coffee, then spend the rest of the morning enjoying stupendous views from the 230m **SkyPoint Observation Deck** (p108).

☀ North of Surfers Paradise, the **Marina Mirage** (p111) by the Broadwater is an upmarket shopping and eating zone with a range of lunch options. Build up an appetite for a two-hour **surfing lesson** (p108) in the afternoon or a dusk **kayaking** (p108) paddle around Chevron Island.

☾ Once the sun sets, the world is your oyster. If you're up for a party, hit the dancefloor at **Elsewhere** (p110) in Surfers – the action begins after midnight.

♥ Best of Brisbane & the Gold Coast

Activities
Australian Kayaking Adventures (p108)

Island Adventures (p108)

Cheyne Horan School of Surf (p108)

Entertainment
Arts Centre Gold Coast (p111)

Markets
Gourmet Farmers Market (p111)

Views
SkyPoint Observation Deck (p108)

Getting There

🚌 **Bus** Premier Motor Service and Greyhound have services to/from Brisbane.

🚆 **Train** TransLink Citytrain services connect Brisbane with Nerang, Robina and Varsity Lakes stations on the Gold Coast (75 minutes).

SOUTH PACIFIC OCEAN

Main Beach

Main Beach Pde

Macarthur Pde

11

Main Beach Pde

MAIN BEACH

Cronin Ave

Sea World Dr

Philip Park

Marina Mirage

2

Island Adventures

5

7

14

Hughes Ave

Tedder Ave

6

Gold Coast Hwy

Waterways Dr

Commodore Dr

The Broadwater

Nerang River

Marine Pde (Gold Coast Hwy)

3

Scarborough St

Lather St

Queen St

SOUTHPORT

Lawson St

White St

Queen St

Meron St

Nerang St

Ferry Rd

High St Sth

Queen St

Minnie St

Benowa Rd

SURFERS PARADISE

Cavill Ave Mall

Surfers Paradise Beach

Cheyne Horan School of Surf

Esplanade

Orchid Ave

Surfers Paradise Blvd

View Ave

Hanlan St

Trickett St

Clifford St

SkyPoint Observation Deck

Hamilton Ave

Elkhorn Ave

Cavill Ave

Ferry Ave

Ferry Ave

Cypress Ave

Remembrance Dr

Norfolk Ave

Pine Ave

River Dr

Budds Beach

Paradise Island

Peninsular Dr

Watson Esp

Admiralty Dr

Thomas Dr

Stanhill Dr

Chevron Island

Stanhill Dr

Nerang River

Ferry Rd

Bundall Rd

Crombie Ave

Cotlew St E

Stanhill Dr

Southport Golf Club

Slatyer Ave

1 km
0.5 mile

For reviews see	
◎ Sights	p108
⊗ Eating	p108
⊗ Drinking	p110
☆ Entertainment	p111
🛍 Shopping	p111

Sights

SkyPoint
Observation Deck   VIEWPOINT

1 ◎ Map p106, D8

Surfers Paradise's best sight is best observed from your beach towel, but for an eagle-eye view of the coast and hinterland, zip up to this 230m-high observation deck near the top of Q1, one of the world's notably tall buildings. You can also tackle the **SkyPoint Climb** (adult/child from $74/54) up the spire to a height of 270m. (www.skypoint.com.au; Level 77, Q1 Bldg, Hamilton Ave, Surfers Paradise; adult/child/family $24/14/62; ☺7.30am-8.30pm Sun-Thu, to 11.30pm Fri & Sat)

Island Adventures   WHALE WATCHING

2 ◎ Map p106, D1

Gawp at wildlife and the Broadwater's sprawling McMansions on this catamaran cruise that includes water sports and a BBQ lunch on McLaren's Landing Eco Resort. (☎07-5532 2444; www.goldcoastadventures.com.au; Mariner's

☑ Top Tip
Up, up and Away
Take a sunrise flight over the Gold Coast with **Balloon Down Under** (☎07-5500 4797; www.balloondownunder.com; 1hr flight adult/child $279/225), ending with a champagne breakfast.

Cove, 60-70 Sea World Dr, Main Beach; cruises incl lunch adult/child $129/69)

Australian
Kayaking Adventures   KAYAKING

3 ◎ Map p106, B1

Paddle out to underrated South Stradbroke Island, or take a dusk paddle around Chevron Island in the calm canals behind Surfers. (☎0412 940 135; www.australiankayakingadventures.com.au; half-day tours adult/child $85/75, sunset tours $55/45)

Cheyne Horan
School of Surf   SURFING

4 ◎ Map p106, D8

Learn to carve up the waves at this school, run by former pro surfer Cheyne Horan. Multilesson packages reduce the cost. (☎1800 227 873; www.cheynehoran.com.au; 2hr lesson $49; ☺10am & 2pm)

Eating

Peter's Fish Market   SEAFOOD $

5 ✖ Map p106, D1

A no-nonsense fish market–cum–fish and chip shop selling fresh and cooked seafood. It's fresh from the trawlers, in all shapes and sizes, and at great prices. Kitchen opens at noon. (☎07-5591 7747; www.petersfish.com.au; 120 Sea World Dr, Main Beach; meals $9-16; ☺9am-7.30pm)

Pier

MODERN AUSTRALIAN, PIZZA $$

An easy but super-stylish, marina-side spot (see **14** Map p106, D1), with upstairs and downstairs seating, both perfect for yachtie views. The mostly European staff is winning and the menu is flexible. Wood-fired pizzas can be combined with arancini (which get their own menu), or there are small and large dishes that tick a number of culinary boxes without being faddish. (07-5527 0472; www.piermarinamirage.com.au; Ground fl, Marina Mirage, 74 Sea World Dr, Main Beach; pizzas $18-24; noon-11.30pm)

Bar Chico

MODERN AUSTRALIAN $$

6 Map p106, D3

A welcome addition to the Tedder strip, this dark and moody European-style bar does fabulous cheese and charcuterie plates, fish or meat tapas-style dishes and big, beguiling salads. Displays a chef-like attention to detail, with in-house fermenting and curing, and lots of high-end ingredients. Wine is similarly thoughtful, with some particularly nice Spanish drops. (07-5532 9111; www.barchico.com.au; 26-30 Tedder Ave, Main Beach; dishes $12-22; 4pm-midnight Mon-Wed, from noon Thu-Sun)

Providore

CAFE $$

Floor-to-ceiling windows rimmed with Italian mineral-water bottles, inverted desk lamps dangling from the ceiling, good-looking Euro tourists, wines by the glass, perfect patisserie goods,

Whale watching

cheese fridges, and baskets overflowing with fresh produce: this excellent deli-cafe gets a lot of things right. Located in the Marina Mirage (see **14** Map p106, D1) (07-5532 9390; www.providoremirage.com.au; Marina Mirage, 74 Sea World Dr, Main Beach; mains $16-29; 7am-6pm)

Vie Bar & Restaurant

MODERN ITALIAN $$

7 Map p106, D1

The most intimate of the Versace restaurants also happens to have the best marina views. Dishes here are stylishly plated and properly sauced (oh, those seafood reductions); the staff is lovely;

CHAMELEONSEYE/SHUTTERSTOCK ©

and it's far from extravagantly priced. Don't miss the signature spanner-crab lasagne – a light and flavourful variant of a classic as ever there could be. (07-5509 8000; www.palazzoversace.com. au; Ground fl, Palazzo Versace, 94 Sea World Dr, Main Beach; mains $29-40; noon-3pm & 6-10pm Fri-Mon;)

Bumbles Café

CAFE $$

8 Map p106, C6

This gorgeous spot – a converted house (actually, at one stage, a brothel) – is the place for breakfast, sweet treats and coffee. It comprises a series of rooms, from the pink Princess Room (perfect for afternoon tea) to a library. Serves up some very desirable cakes. (07-5538 6668; www.bumblescafe. com; 21 River Dr, Budds Beach, Surfers Paradise; mains $14-24; 7.30am-4pm)

Drinking

Elsewhere

CLUB

9 Map p106, D7

A Saturday Night Fever–style dance floor always bodes well for good times, and this little bar-to-club venue features DJs who know their electronica, including cracking live sets from the soon-to-be-famous. Crowds are cooler than elsewhere, but it's a friendly, conversation-filled place, until DJs seriously turn up the volume. (07-5592 6880; www.elsewherebar.com; 23 Cavill Ave, Surfers Paradise; 9pm-4am Thu-Sun)

Black Coffee Lyrics

BAR, CAFE

10 Map p106, D7

Upstairs and hidden in an unexpected location – within a nondescript arcade – this is the antithesis to Surfers shiny. Filled with vintage furniture and bordering on grungy, it's a dark oasis where locals come for coffee and tapas-style dishes, for steaks, and for bourbon, boutique brews and espresso martinis until late. Weekend breakfasts are hearty and there's the option of beer or Bloody Marys from 10am. (0402 189 437; www.facebook. com/blackcoffeelyrics; 40/3131 Surfers Paradise Blvd, Surfers Paradise; 5pm-late Tue-Fri, from 8am Sat & Sun)

Southport Surf Lifesaving Club

CLUB

11 Map p106, D2

This beautiful, airy pavilion-style club has spectacular views. The deck

---

Understand
Schoolies on the Loose

Every year in November, thousands of teenagers flock to Surfers Paradise to celebrate the end of their high-school education in a three-week party known as Schoolies Week. Although local authorities have stepped in to regulate excesses, boozed-up and drug-addled teens are still the norm. It's not pretty. For more info, see www. schoolies.com.

is open early for coffee, or head here for lazy beery afternoons. It's one of the only places open late north of Surfers. (www.sslsc.com.au; Macarthur Pde; ⊙6.30am–midnight)

Beergarden
BAR

12 🚇 Map p106, D7

Not so much a garden – more of a black-painted beer barn with a long balcony overlooking Cavill Ave that's awash with backpackers and students. Steel yourself with a few cold ones on the balcony before you hit the clubs, or catch the regular bevy of live bands and live UFC (mixed marital arts) and boxing matches. Good times. (www.surfersbeergarden.com.au; Cavill Ave, Surfers Paradise; ⊙noon–5am)

Entertainment

Arts Centre Gold Coast
THEATRE, CINEMA

13 ⭐ Map p106, B7

A bastion of culture and civility beside the Nerang River, the Arts Centre has two cinemas, a restaurant, a bar, the Gold Coast City Gallery and a 1200-seat theatre, which regularly hosts impressive productions (comedy, jazz, opera, kids' concerts etc). (📞07-5588 4000; www.theartscentregc.com.au; 135 Bundall Rd, Surfers Paradise; ⊙box office 8am–9pm Mon–Fri, to 9pm Sat, 11am–7pm Sun)

Shopping

Gourmet Farmers Market
MARKET

On Saturday mornings, the open spaces of the Marina Mirage mall (see 14 🔒 Map p106, D1) fill with stalls selling seasonal fruit and veg, baked goods, pickles, oils, vinegars, seafood, pasta and more, all from small-scale producers and makers. (📞07-5555 6400; www.facebook.com/MarinaMirageFarmersMarket; Marina Mirage, 74 Sea World Dr, Main Beach; ⊙7-11am Sat)

Marina Mirage
SHOPPING CENTRE

14 🔒 Map p106, D1

Half the fun might be saying the name, but this airy, reassuringly small-scaled mall has an eclectic range of shops, reliable services, and some great eating options; an excellent farmers market is held here on Saturday mornings. (📞07-5555 6400; www.marinamirage.com.au; 74 Sea World Dr, Main Beach; ⊙10am–6pm)

Explore

Burleigh Heads & Currumbin

The super-chilled surfie enclave of Burleigh has long been a family favourite, but is currently having its moment in the sun. The town's gently retro vibe and palpable youthful energy epitomise both the Gold Coast's timeless appeal and its new, increasingly interesting, spirit. You'll find some of the region's best cafes and restaurants dotted around its little grid.

The Sights in a Day

 Start the day with a freshly baked croissant at **Paddock Bakery** (p117) or a filling chia-bowl at **Borough Barista** (p119).

Spend the day wildlife-spotting in the surrounding area. **David Fleay Wildlife Park** (p116), 3km from Burleigh Heads, gives you the chance to explore the walking tracks through mangroves and possibly catch a wildlife show. Alternatively, make your way down the coast for a visit to the native animals at **Currumbin Wildlife Sanctuary** (p116), stopping off at **Elephant Rock Cafe** (p118) for lunch.

On the way back to Burleigh, pop into Mick Fanning's **Balter** (p120) brewery for a tasting paddle, then to **Harry's Steak Bistro** (p119) for hearty fare, or **Finders Keepers** (p119) for tapas-style cuisine.

Best of Brisbane & the Gold Coast

Activities

Federation Walk (p117)

Currumbin Wildlife Sanctuary (p116)

Gold Coast Oceanway (p117)

Drinking

Balter (p120)

Cambus Wallace (p120)

Burleigh Brewing Company (p121)

For Kids

Currumbin Wildlife Sanctuary (p116)

Getting There

🚌 **Bus** Premier Motor Service links Burleigh Heads to various points north and south, including Byron Bay ($29 to $35). Surfside Buslines runs local bus 702 that links Gold Coast Airport to Southport, stopping at Burleigh Heads on the way.

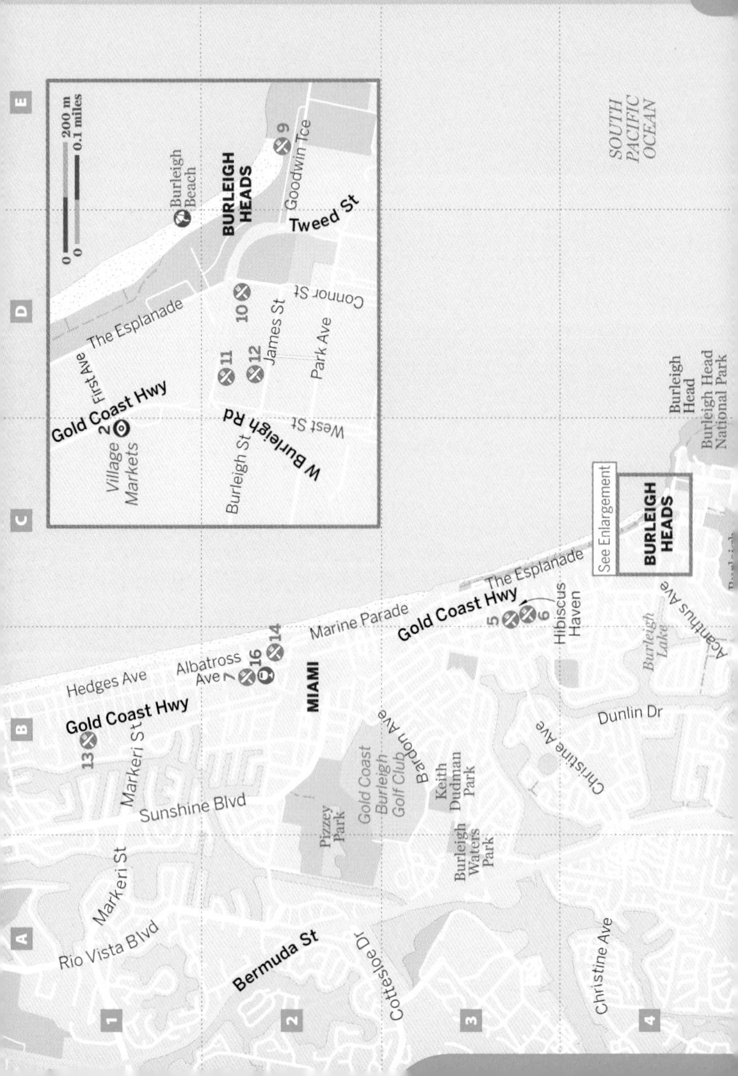

SOUTH
PACIFIC
OCEAN

E

200 m
0.1 miles

0
0

Burleigh
Beach

**BURLEIGH
HEADS**

9

Tweed St

Goodwin Tce

D

10

Connor St

James St

Park Ave

11 12

West St

Gold Coast Hwy

First Ave

The Esplanade

W Burleigh Rd

Burleigh St

2

Village
Markets

C

Burleigh
Head

Burleigh Head
National Park

See Enlargement

**BURLEIGH
HEADS**

Acanthus Ave

Burleigh
Lake

The Esplanade

Gold Coast Hwy

Marine Parade

5   6

Hibiscus
Haven

Dunlin Dr

Hedges Ave

Albatross
Ave
7   16 14

MIAMI

Gold Coast Hwy

13

Markeri St

Bardon Ave

Gold
Coast
Burleigh
Golf Club

Keith
Dudman
Park

Burleigh
Waters
Park

Christine Ave

Christine Ave

B

Sunshine Blvd

Pizzey
Park

Dunlin Dr

A

Markeri St

Rio Vista Blvd

Bermuda St

Cottesloe Dr

Christine Ave

1   2   3   4

Tallebudgera Beach

Gold Coast Hwy

Palm Beach

Currumbin Beach

Pacific Parade

⊗8

⊙1

CURRUMBIN

Currumbin Wildlife Sanctuary

TUGUN

Tugun Currumbin Rd

Gold Coast Hwy

Thrower Dr

Durringan St

Pacific Hwy

Currumbin Creek Rd

15

⊙

⊙4

Currumbin Creek

Nineteenth Ave

Palm Beach Ave

Mallawa Dr

K P McGrath Dr

ELANORA

Ikina Rd

Tallebudgera Environmental Park

Tallebudgera Dr

David Fleay Wildlife Park

⊙3

West Burleigh Rd

Pacific Hwy

Nineteenth Ave

Kudge Park

Tallebudgera Creek Rd

Tallebudgera Creek

Reedy Creek Rd

⊡17

Bermuda St

Pacific Hwy

For reviews see

⊙⊗⊗⊡ Sights		p116
	Eating	p117
	Drinking	p120

Ⓝ

0 ———— 1 mile
0 ———— 2 km

A B C D E

Sights

Currumbin Wildlife Sanctuary
WILDLIFE RESERVE

1  Map p114, E8

This nicely restrained, old-style operation includes Australia's biggest rainforest aviary, where you can hand-feed a technicolour blur of rainbow lorikeets. There's also kangaroo feeding, photo ops with koalas and crocodiles, reptile shows and Aboriginal dance displays. Entry is reduced after 3pm, and there's often an adults-at-kids-prices special during school holidays. (☑1300 886 511, 07-5534 1266; www.cws.org.au; 28 Tomewin St, Currumbin; adult/child/family $49/35/133; ⊘8am-5pm)

Village Markets
MARKET

2  Map p114, C1

A long-running market that highlights local designers, makers and collectors, with fashion and lifestyle stalls, lots of live music and a strong local following. (☑0487 711 850; www.thevillagemarkets.co; Burleigh Heads State School, 1750 Gold Coast Hwy, Burleigh Heads; ⊘8.30am-1pm 1st & 3rd Sun of month)

David Fleay Wildlife Park
WILDLIFE RESERVE

3  Map p114, C5

Opened by the doctor who first succeeded in breeding platypuses, this wildlife park has 4km of walk-

DAVID BOSTOCK/SHUTTERSTOCK ©

Rainbow lorikeets at Currumbin Wildlife Sanctuary

ing tracks through mangroves and rainforest, and plenty of informative native wildlife shows throughout the day. It's around 3km inland from Burleigh Heads. (📞07-5576 2411; www.npsr.qld.gov.au/parks/david-fleay; cnr Loman Lane & West Burleigh Rd, West Burleigh; adult/child/family $22/10/55; ⏱9am-5pm)

Currumbin Rock Pools SWIMMING

 4 Map p114, D8

These natural swimming holes are a cool spot during the hot summer months, and feature grassy banks for kids to run around and rocky ledges from which teenagers can plummet. It's 14km up Currumbin Creek Rd from the coast. (Currumbin Creek Rd, Currumbin Valley)

Eating

Paddock Bakery BAKERY $

 5 Map p114, C3

An antique wood-fired oven sits in the heart of this beautiful old weatherboard cottage and turns out wonderful bread, croissants, granola and pastries. The semi-sourdough doughnuts have a devoted fan base, as do the Nutella doughboats – spherical-shaped to fit more goo. There's a full breakfast and lunch menu, too, as well as top coffee and cold-pressed juices. (📞0419 652 221; www.paddockbakery.com; Hibiscus Haven, Miami; dishes $9-17; ⏱7.30am-2.30pm)

 Top Tip

Top Tips

The Gold Coast has a couple of excellent walking trails. **Federation Walk** (www.federationwalk.org) is a pretty 3.7km trail through patches of fragrant littoral rainforest, running parallel to one of the world's most beautiful strips of surf beach, starting and ending at Sea World. Along the way it connects to the **Gold Coast Oceanway**, which heads 36km to Coolangatta.

Burleigh Social CAFE $

 6 Map p114, C3

This backstreet cafe has a party vibe from early morning at its picnic-table seating. There's paleo granola or the big paleo breakfast (salmon, bacon or ham with kale, eggs and avocado) or nicely done versions of Australian cafe staples such as smashed avocado, eggs on sourdough and bacon-and-egg rolls. Brisket subs and veggie burgers take it into lunch. (2 Hibiscus Haven, Burleigh Heads; dishes $12-19; ⏱6am-2pm)

Sparrow Eating House MODERN AUSTRALIAN $

 7 Map p114, B2

This lovely, clean-lined monochrome industrial space with green accents has a low-key glamour and a kitchen that loves what it does. Come for a casual lunch of spring gnocchi

Understand
Goldie's Best Surf Breaks

The Gold Coast possesses some of the longest, hollowest and best waves in the world, and is lauded for its epic consistency. The creation of the **Superbank** – a sand bar that's formed as part of anti-erosion efforts and stretches 2km from the Queensland–New South Wales border up to Kirra – has made for a decade of even better waves, even more often.

Snapper Rocks A highly advanced point break at Coolangatta's far south.

Greenmount Classic beach break that benefits from a southerly swell.

Kirra Beautiful beach break; long barrels that are some of the world's best.

Burleigh Heads Strong currents and boulders to watch out for, but a perfect break that's more often on than not.

The Spit One of north Goldie's stalwarts, this peaky beach break can work even when the surf is small.

with hazelnuts and herbs; enjoy a blood-orange margarita and some tequila prawns; or pop in for a glass of small-producer wine. (☏07-5575 3330; www.sparroweatinghouse.com.au; 2/32 Lavarack Rd, Nobby Beach; sharing dishes $11-22; ☺5pm-midnight Wed-Fri, from 7am Sat & Sun)

Elephant Rock Café   MODERN AUSTRALIAN, CAFE $$

 8   Map p114, E7

On the refreshingly underdeveloped Currumbin beachfront you'll find this breezy, two-tier cafe, which morphs from beachy by day into surprisingly chic at night. Great ocean views and even better Mooloolaba spanner-crab salad and 'green' risotto. (☏07-5598

2133; www.elephantrock.com.au; 776 Pacific Pde, Currumbin; mains $28-35; ☺7am-late Tue-Sat, to 5pm Sun & Mon)

Rick Shores   MODERN ASIAN $$

 9   Map p114, E2

Feet-in-the-sand dining can often play it safe, and while this Modern Asian newcomer sends out absolute crowd-pleasing dishes, it's also pleasingly inventive. The space is all about the view, the sound of the nearby waves, the salty breeze and communal-table conviviality. Serves are huge, which can allay the menu price if you're not dining solo and are into sharing. (☏07-5630 6611; www.rickshores.com.au; 43 Goodwin Tce, Burleigh Heads; mains $32-52; ☺noon-11pm Tue-Sun)

Justin Lane Pizzeria & Bar

PIZZA $$

10 Map p114, D2

One of the seminal players in Burleigh's food and drinking scene, Justin Lane has now colonised most of an old shopping arcade. Yes, the fun stretches upstairs, downstairs and across the hall. Great pizzas, simple but flavour-packed pasta dishes and possibly the coast's best regional Italian wine list make it a must, even if you're not here for the party vibe. (☎ 07-5576 8517; www.justinlane.com.au; 1708 Gold Coast Hwy, Burleigh Heads; pizzas $19-24; ⏲ 5pm-late)

Harry's Steak Bistro

STEAK $$

11 Map p114, D2

Don't misread the menu – a mix and match steak-and-sauce affair, plus unlimited fries – as belonging to a chain restaurant. Harry's, a stylish, sparse paean to 'beef, booze and banter', is super-serious about its steaks, with each accredited with the name of its farm and region. (☎ 07-5576 8517; www.harryssteakbistro.com.au; 1744 Gold Coast Hwy, Burleigh Heads; mains $20-40; ⏲ 5-11pm Wed & Thu, noon-11pm Fri-Sun)

Finders Keepers

MODERN AUSTRALIAN $$

12 Map p114, D2

This dark, stylish restaurant feels like it's been transported from Sydney's Woollahra or Melbourne's South Yarra, but the friendly young staff is pure Burleigh. Similarly, the tapas-style dishes are a mix of sophistication (foie-gras parfait and poached scallop mornay) and health-conscious coastal casual (ancient grain salad, and salmon on buckwheat and seasonal greens with a sea-vegetable butter sauce). (☎ 07-5659 1643; www.finderskeepersbar.com.au; 49 James St; mains $16-29; ⏲ 4-10pm Tue-Fri, 7am-11pm Sat & Sun)

Glenelg Public House

STEAK $$

13 Map p114, B1

A passionate little place, this atmospheric eating and drinking den uses premium produce and has a light hand with accompaniments. The epic steak list ($22 to $68, sharing $80 to $90) takes in local breeds, the best of New Zealand and New South Wales tablelands and both grass- and grain-fed cuts. There's also an 'early tea' dinner

 Local Life

Borough Barista

It's all cool tunes and friendly vibes at **Borough Barista** (Map p114, D1; 14 Esplanade, Burleigh Heads; mains $5-19; ⏲ 5.30am-2.30pm), this little open-walled espresso shack. Join local surfers for their dawn piccolo lattes and post-surf for a chia bowl or breakfast salad on a footpath bench. Lunches revolve around good proteins with burgers or big salads.

special before 6.30pm. (☑07-5575 2284; www.theglenelgpublichouse.com.au; 2460 Gold Coast Hwy, Mermaid Beach; mains $22-32; ⏱5pm-midnight Mon-Thu, from noon Fri-Sun)

BSKT Cafe MODERN AUSTRALIAN $$

14 Map p114, B2

This satisfyingly industrial cafe is 100m from the beach, but that's far from its only charm. It's the brainchild of four buddies whose focus is organic produce, and the dishes and service punch well above cafe level. Vegans and paleos will be equally at home here, as will kids (there's a fenced play area) and yogis (there's an upstairs yoga school). (☑07-5526 6565; www.bskt.com.au; 4 Lavarack Ave, Mermaid Beach;

 Top Tip

Cafe Style

Cafe opening hours often come as a shock, with many opening as early as 5am, and virtually all of them pumping by 7am. Local culinary quirks are all about the climate and the coast's fitness ethos. Don't miss the surfers' delight, a Brazilian açaí bowl – essentially a thick smoothie topped with granola or nuts; iced lattes made with macadamia or coconut milk; and poke, a Hawaiian–Japanese fusion of marinated raw fish, rice or quinoa and vegetables.

mains $10-27; ⏱7am-4pm Mon-Thu, to 10pm Fri & Sat, to 5pm Sun;)

Drinking

Balter BREWERY

15 Map p114, D8

Local surf star Mick Fanning (the man who punched a shark, right?) and his fellow circuit legends Joel Parkinson, Bede Durbidge and Josh Kerr are all partners in this wonderful new brewery, hidden away at the back of a Currumbin industrial estate. Come and sample the already sought-after Balter XPA or a special such as the German-style Keller pilsner. (☑07-5525 6916; www.balter.com.au; 14 Traders Way, Currumbin; tasting paddles $12; ⏱3-9pm Fri, 1-8pm Sat & Sun)

Cambus Wallace COCKTAIL BAR

16 Map p114, B2

Dark, moody, maritime-themed bar that attracts a good-looking but relaxed local crew. Settle in with something from its long, long list of bottled beer and cider, or try a Gold Coast take on cocktail classics (there's no Dark 'n' Stormy but a coconut, lime and rum Maiden Voyage could not be better suited to the climate). (www.thecambuswallace.com.au; 4/2237 Gold Coast Hwy, Nobby Beach; ⏱5pm-midnight Tue-Thu, from 4pm Fri-Sun)

Currumbin Rock Pools (p117)

Burleigh Brewing Company

BREWERY

17 🍺 Map p114, A5

Hang out in this light, woody and blokey space with fellow beer lovers. There's live music and local food trucks, not to mention a 24-tap line-up of Burleigh brews, including their main line and pilot project beers. Tours run on Wednesday nights mid-month and need to be booked through the website. (☏07-5593 6000; www. burleighbrewing.com.au; 17a Ern Harley Dr, Burleigh Heads; monthly tours $50; ⊙3-6pm Wed & Thu, to 8.30pm Fri, 2-8pm Sun)

Black Hops Brewing

BREWERY

Around the corner from the Burleigh Social (see 6 ❌ Map p114, C3), the Black Hops boys run a friendly and fun tap room where you can enjoy a paddle or whatever craft delight they've currently got on tap. There are eight poetically named beers – from the Bitter Fun pale ale to the Flash Bang white IPA – to choose from, or you can purchase whatever they have bottled. (www.blackhops.com.au; 15 Gardenia Grove, Burleigh Heads; ⊙10am-6pm Mon-Fri, noon-4pm Sat)

Local Life
An Evening in Coolangatta

Getting There

Greyhound (📞1300 473 946; www.greyhound.com.au) runs to Brisbane and beyond, while **Premier Motor Service** (📞13 34 10; www.premierms.com.au) heads as far north as Cairns. Coaches stop on Wharf St.

A down-to-earth beach town on Queensland's far southern border, 'Coolie' has quality surf beaches, including the legendary Superbank, and a tight-knit, very real community that makes it feel less touristy than it otherwise could. Follow the board-walk north around Kirra Point for another beautiful long stretch of beach, sometimes challenging surf, and locally loved indie-atmosphere cafes and bars.

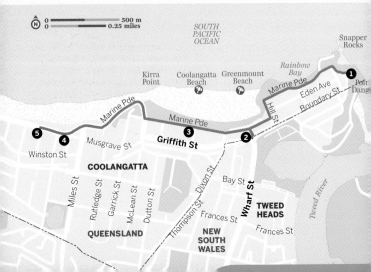

1 Point Danger

The headland of Point Danger, sitting between Coolangatta and Tweed Heads, marks the border between Queensland and New South Wales. The Brutalist concrete tower that marks the spot (and the cardinal directions) is, despite its sculptural aspirations, a working lighthouse. Once a laser, it's now a tried-and-true electric beacon. There are amazing views from here both ways along the coast. Watch the sunset over the horizon before heading on to Coolangatta's handful of bars and pubs.

2 Eddie's Grub House

A totally old-school rock-and-roll bar, with dirty blues and best-of rock soundtrack, **Eddie's** (☑07-5599 2177; www.eddiesgrubhouse.com; 171 Griffith St; ⏱noon-10.30pm Tue-Thu & Sun, to midnight Fri & Sat) is emblematic of the new Gold Coast: indie, ironic and really fun. Yes, there's grub to be had, and Eddie's 'dive bar comfort food' is exactly that. But this is a place for drinking, dancing, chatting and chilling (as they say themselves).

3 Coolangatta Hotel

The hub of Coolangatta's sometimes boisterous nocturnal scene, this huge **pub** (www.thecoolyhotel.com.au; cnr Marine Pde & Warner St; ⏱10am-late), right across from the beach, pumps with live bands (Grinspoon, The Rubens), sausage sizzles, pool comps, trivia nights, acoustic jam nights, surprisingly sophisticated pub-meal deals (pasta and rosé, anyone?) – basically, the works. Big Sunday sessions.

4 Bread 'n' Butter

Head upstairs to the **Bread 'n' Butter** (☑07-5599 4666; www.breadnbutter.com.au; 76 Musgrave St; tapas $16-27, pizzas $21-25; ⏱5.30pm-late) balcony, where mood lighting and chilled tunes make this tapas bar perfect for a drink, a wood-fired pizza or some tapas (or perhaps all three). Even the wood in the oven is local – it's gum from Currumbin. DJs spin on Friday and Saturday nights.

5 Tupe Aloha

Tipalowe Oberman's **tiki bar** (☑07-5536 4870; www.facebook.com/TupeAloha; 1 Musgrave St, Kirra; ⏱3-11pm Mon-Thu, to midnight Fri-Sun) is filled with her dad's art and her grandparents' furniture. Come for the Mexican-via-Pacific-Rim snacks (there are great weeknight deals on tacos and drinks) and stay for the cocktails (yes, they come with umbrellas) and DJs.

The Best of
Brisbane &
the Gold Coast

Brisbane & the Gold Coast's Best Walks

Brisbane & the Gold Coast's Best...

Boardwalk through South Bank Parklands (p46)
PETRONILO G DANGOY JR/SHUTTERSTOCK ©

Best Walks
CBD to South Bank

🏃 The Walk

This leisurely two-hour walk begins conveniently at Central Station and meanders along the Brisbane River across the Goodwill Bridge to South Bank, stopping at heritage sites and the greenery of the botanical gardens and South Bank Parklands.

Start Central Station

Finish King George Sq

Length 5km; two hours

🍴 Take a Break

The Gallery of Modern Art deserves more than an hour of your time, so **GOMA Cafe Bistro** (p45), its casual on-site eatery, is the perfect place to take a break. The indoor-outdoor dining space serves high-quality burgers, salads and modern bistro mains, with both breakfast and lunch served on the weekends.

Shrine of Remembrance

HOLGS/GETTY IMAGES ©

❶ Shrine of Remembrance

Cross Ann St south of Central Station to the elegant **Shrine of Remembrance** above the northern edge of Anzac Sq, with its bulbous boab trees and wandering ibises.

❷ Post Office Sq

At the southern side of the square, scale one of the pedestrian bridges over Adelaide St to manicured **Post Office Sq**. The square is fronted at its southern end by Brisbane's stately stone GPO.

❸ St Stephen's Cathedral

Take the alley between the wings of the post office through to Elizabeth St. Cross the road and stick your head into beautiful white-stone **St Stephen's Cathedral**.

❹ Eagle St Pier

Walk through the courtyard behind the cathedral until reaching Charlotte St. Take a left, cross Eagle St and duck through **Eagle St Pier** on the river.

❺ City Botanic Gardens

At Edward and Alice Sts, detour through the **City Botanic Gardens** (p28). Cast an eye across the river to the Kangaroo Point cliffs, then skirt around the back of the Brisbane Riverstage to the pedestrian-only Goodwill Bridge: check out HMAS *Diamantina* in the Queensland Maritime Museum to your left.

❻ South Bank Parklands

From here, jag north into the **South Bank Parklands** (p46), where you can chill out on sandy Streets Beach, ride the Wheel of Brisbane or browse the shops and cafes of Stanley St Plaza.

❼ Gallery of Modern Art

If time is your friend, detour to the outstanding **Gallery of Modern Art** (p44). Otherwise, cross Victoria Bridge back into central Brisbane. Just south of the gorgeous Treasury Casino building on William St, an unnamed alley cuts through to George St.

❽ City Hall

Continue along Albert St, cross Queen Street Mall and then Adelaide St into King George Sq, where the towering **City Hall** (p24) beckons with its commanding clock-tower views.

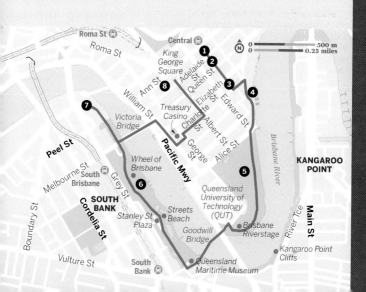

Best Walks
Central Brisbane

🏃 The Walk

This Central Brisbane stroll can take as little as an hour, but allow half a day to enjoy some shopping and relaxation in the city parks. It will take you through some of Central Brisbane's main retail streets and to some of its coolest arts venues.

Start Roma Street Parkland

Finish QUT Art Museum

Length 4.5km

✕ Take a Break

Central Brisbane has its share of cosy cafes but it's hard to beat **Felix for Goodness** (p31) with its arty laneway locale, industrial fit-out, strong espresso and effortlessly cool vibe. Another nearby option is **Strauss** (p31), offering seriously good coffee, pastries and a locavore menu of creative salads, thick-cut toasted sandwiches and upgraded classics such as French toast paired with lemon curd and labna.

Queen St Mall

❶ Roma Street Parkland

Start with a morning stroll in the lovely **Roma St Parkland** (p28), one of the world's largest subtropical urban gardens and a satisfying maze. Look out for the Old Windmill on Wickham Tce – reputedly the oldest surviving building in Queensland (1828).

❷ Spring Hill Baths

It's a short walk north to **Spring Hill Baths** (p30), one of the oldest public baths in the southern hemisphere, encircled by cute timber change rooms. If you're not tempted for a dip, continue east along Boundary St and track south towards Anzac Sq.

❸ Noosa Chocolate Factory

Duck down Adelaide St and into **Noosa Chocolate Factory** (p38) to sample some of Queensland's best chocolate.

❹ Metro Arts

Head down Edward St to **Metro Arts** (p37) where you might find some of Brisbane's creative talent performing.

❺ Folio Books

Continue just a little further along Edward St to **Folio Books** (p39), with an eclectic, sophisticated collection covering everything from Canberra politics and Queensland modernism, to international art, gastronomy, design and fiction.

❻ Queen St Mall

Head back and turn left into Queen St where you'll find the heart of Brisbane's retail action in the **Queen St Mall**, a busy, pedestrian strip lined with shopping malls and historic arcades, global high-street chains and the city's two main department stores.

❼ Jan Powers Farmers Market

If it's a Wednesday, stock up on artisan foods for a picnic at the popular **Jan Powers Farmers Market** (p31).

❽ Record Exchange

If it's not a Wednesday, check out the astounding collection of vinyl, CDs, DVDs, posters and other rock memorabilia at the **Record Exchange** (p39) on Adelaide St.

❾ QUT Art Museum

Take a stroll down George St, passing Parliament House (free tours at 2pm when parliament is sitting) and skirting the botanic gardens before reaching the Queensland University of Technology city campus. Pop into the free **QUT Art Museum** (p30) to see what exhibitions are on.

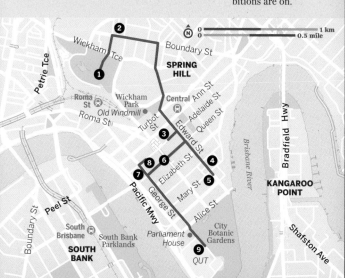

Best
Food

Brisbane's food scene is flourishing – a fact not lost on the nation's food critics and switched-on gluttons. From Mod Oz degustations to curbside food trucks, the city offers an increasingly competent, confident array of culinary highs. Particularly notable is the growing number of eateries fusing high-end culinary sophistication with an easy, casual vibe that is indelibly Brisbane. Hungry? You should be.

Food Trucks

There's an ever-growing number of food vans roaming city streets, serving up good-quality fast food, from tacos, ribs, wings and burgers, to wood-fired pizza, Brazilian hot dogs and Malaysian saté. You'll find a list of Brisbane food trucks (with respective menus) at www.bnefoodtrucks.com.au. From Tuesday to Sunday, Fish Lane hosts **Eating at Wandering Cooks**, a rotating mix of quality food trucks and stalls open for lunch and dinner.

Cooking Courses

Consider booking a course at one of the city's cooking schools, where most courses run for a few hours. Fortitude Valley is home to the James St Cooking School (p69), conveniently located above the gourmet James Street Market. A little further out in Newstead is the **Golden Pig Cooking School & Cafe** (07-3666 0884; www.goldenpig.com.au; 38 Ross St, Newstead; 4hr cooking class $165; cafe 7.30am-noon Mon, to 2pm Tue-Fri; 300, 302, 305), run by an accomplished chef whose resume lists some of Australia's most respected restaurants.

Generally, courses should be booked at least a week in advance

DAVID AHN/GETTY IMAGES ©

Restaurants

Urbane One of only two three-hatted heavy-weights in Brisbane and an eight-course degustation menu. (p33)

1889 Enoteca Roman-inspired dishes such as pork-and-fennel-sausage gnocchi served with true Italian elegance. (p99)

Billykart West End Dishes are beautifully textured and flavoured at this slick but casual eatery where chilli-spiked Aussie-Asian eggs are a hit. (p56)

Gauge Sophisticated, contemporary fare with a provocative edge; try the savoury-sweet black garlic bread. (p55)

Longtime Try soft-shell-crab *bao* with Asian slaw at this buzzing, alleyway favourite peddling vibrant, classic-meets-contemporary Thai. (p71)

Eat Street Markets

Les Bubbles This sassy steakhouse serves up superb steak frites with bottomless fries and salad. (p71)

Stokehouse Q Linen-lined tables, sophisticated fare and dreamy views of the river and city skyline. Try the epic dessert, Bombe. (p56)

E'cco Bistro classics get seductive makeovers at this two-hatted classic. Save room for just-baked choc-chip cookies. (p72)

Julius Wood-fired pizzas and perfect pasta in a buzzing, contemporary setting. (p55)

Cha Cha Char Linen-tabled steakhouse, famed for its wood-fired slabs of premium Australian beef. (p33)

Cafes & Quick Bites

King Arthur Cafe Top-notch local produce turned into inspired breakfast and lunch bites. (p66)

Miel Container Burgers lauded by Australia's MasterChef judges. (p31)

Tinderbox A tucked-away spot with gorgeous pizzas and a sophisticated Valley crowd. (p72)

Sourced Grocer Regional ingredients can be both eaten and bought at this post-industrial cafe-cum-providore. Comforting cabbage pancakes. (p85)

Morning After An upbeat, airy space offering fresh takes on classic cafe grub. (p54)

Felix for Goodness Arty laneway locale, industrial fit-out and effortlessly cool vibe. (p31)

Worth a Trip

The hugely popular **Eat Street Markets** (☎07-3358 2500; www.eatstreet markets.com; 99 MacArthur Ave, Hamilton; admission adult/child $2.50/free, meals from $10; ⏰4-10pm Fri & Sat; ⛴Bretts Wharf) is the city's hipsterish take on the night street-food market, with a maze of upcycled shipping containers pumping out everything from freshly shucked oysters to smoky American barbecue and Turkish gözleme, to the sound of live bands.

Best
Activities

Brisbane's subtropical climate encourages physical activity, with a slew of activities ranging from cycling and rock climbing, to swimming, kayaking and more. In many cases, these activities offer the best views of the city itself, making them sightseeing experiences in themselves. You'll find a plethora of excellent art and heritage walking trails around town at www.brisbane.qld.gov.au/facilities -recreation/sports-leisure/walking/walking-trails.

CATHY FINCH/GETTY IMAGES ©

Biking Brisbane

Despite its hilliness, Brisbane is one of Australia's most bike-friendly cities, with more than 900km of bike paths, including tracks along the Brisbane River. A good starter takes you from the City Botanic Gardens, across the Goodwill Bridge and out to the University of Queensland. For information on cycling routes and events around town, check out the free, subscription-based website www. cyclingbrisbane.com.au.

Up and Away

Hot-air ballooning is a sensational way to see the city, coast and hinterland. One-hour flights typically take off before dawn so you can see the sun rise over the Pacific Ocean in ethereal silence. Back on land you'll enjoy a champagne breakfast. Operators include **Fly Me to the Moon** (☑07-3423 0400; www.brisbanehotairballooning.com.au; adult/child incl transfers from $250/330) in Brisbane and Balloon Down Under (p108) in Surfers Paradise.

More adventurous travellers can try skydiving. High-adrenaline tandem skydives are on offer from 12,000 feet, naturally landing on the beach. In Brisbane jump with **Skydive Brisbane** (☑1300 663 634; www.skydive.com.au; from $300), on the Gold Coast

☑ **Top Tips**

▶ Brisbane's bike-share program is called **CityCycle** (☑1300 229 253; www. citycycle.com.au; hire per hr/day $2.20/165, 1st 30min free; ⊙24hr). To use it, you will need to subscribe via the website (per day/week $2/11), then hire a bike (additional fee) from any of the 150 stations around town. Make use of the free first 30 minutes per bike and ride from station to station, swapping bikes as you go.

try **Gold Coast Skydive** (☑07-5599 1920; www.gold coastskydive.com.au; 1/78 Musgrave St, Kirra Beach; tandem jumps from $355).

Story Bridge Adventure Climb (p97)

Swimming

Streets Beach Australia's only artificial, inner-city beach, complete with lifeguards, at South Bank. (p46)

Valley Pool Heated outdoor pool and the place to be seen. (p67)

Spring Hill Baths Quaint 130-year-old pool, Brisbane's first. (p30)

Currumbin Rock Pools Natural inland swimming holes with grassy banks. (p117)

Surfing & Kayaking

Australian Kayaking Adventures Paddle out to South Stradbroke or Chevron island. (p108)

Cheyne Horan School of Surf Carve up the waves with former pro surfer Cheyne Horan. (p108)

Climbing

Story Bridge Adventure Climb Two-hour climb scales the southern half of the structure, tak-

ing you 80m above the twisting, muddy Brisbane River. Dawn climbs are run on the last Saturday of the month. (p97)

Riverlife Rock climbing, abseiling, kayaking and inline skating. (p97)

Urban Climb Indoor climbing wall with one of the largest bouldering walls in Australia. (p54)

Pinnacle Sports Climb the Kangaroo Point Cliffs or abseil down. (p101)

Worth a Trip

The 1½-hour **XXXX Brewery Tour** (📞 07-3361 7597; www.xxxx.com.au; cnr Black & Paten Sts, Milton; adult/child $32/18; 🚌 375, 433, 475) demonstrates the factory process and includes a few humidity-beating ales. Tours run four times daily Monday to Friday and nine times Saturday. Also on offer are combined brewery and **Suncorp Stadium tours** (adult/child $48/28) at 10.30am Thursday. There's also an alehouse here if you feel like kicking on.

Best
Nightlife

Brisbane's bar scene has evolved into a sophisticated entity, with sharp, competent drinking holes pouring everything from natural wines and locally made saisons, to G&Ts spiked with native ingredients. The city's live-music scene is equally robust, with cult-status venues in Fortitude Valley, West End and the city itself pumping out impressive local and international talent. Tip: always carry some photo ID.

A Drink with A View

Brisbane's balmy climate and Brisvegas skyline make it the perfect place for rooftop bars, alfresco riverside terraces and boisterous beer gardens. The king of rooftop bars is Eleven (p73), with mesmerising views of slimline city towers and distant Mt Coot-tha. Sazerac Bar (p36) is Brisbane's highest, with commanding city views for spot-the-landmark sessions, while Mr & Mrs G (p36) Riverbar offers well-mixed cocktails, Moroccan details and killer skyscraper and water views.

Gold Coast Clubbing

The Gold Coast is known as a nightlife destination, but beyond its 4am club zones can feel pretty sleepy (possibly because locals are up early to surf). Traditional beer barns and surf clubs are community hubs, but there's a growing number of cosmopolitan wine bars, hip cocktail dens and terrace sundowner venues, especially from Broadbeach down to the NSW border. Beer is taken very seriously, with a number of small breweries and welcoming tap rooms.

☑ Top Tips

▶ Fortitude Valley is known as Brisbane's nightlife central, with acclaimed wine, cocktail and rooftop bars, and thumping clubs, but it's not the only place in town.

▶ Try central Brisbane and South Bank for riverside bars and craft spirits; New Farm for award-winning microbreweries; and Kangaroo Point for a small clutch of cocktail and wine bars.

▶ On the Gold Coast, Surfers Paradise is the place to be.

Bars

Gerard's Bar Enlightening wines, impeccable bar snacks and sharp, new-Brisbane sophistication. (p73)

Maker A pocket-sized wonder with progressive, beautifully crafted libations. (p57)

Bar Alto Languid riverside sessions at a cultured former powerhouse. (p91)

Eleven The king of rooftop bars, with mesmerising views of slimline city towers and distant Mt Coot-tha. (p73)

Gresham Bar An after-work city favourite with handsome heritage features. (p34)

Microbreweries

Newstead Brewing Co Sip suds in the very

warehouse in which they're brewed. (p92)

Green Beacon Brewing Co Award-winning, made-on-site beers with seasonal suds and special releases. (p91)

Burleigh Brewing Company Live music and local food trucks, not to mention a 24-tap line-up of Burleigh brews. (p121)

Balter New brewery owned by surf stars Mick Fanning, Joel Parkinson, Bede Durbidge and Josh Kerr. (p120)

Cocktail & Wine Bars

APO Single-batch bottled cocktails with intriguing twists. (p73)

Canvas Club Clever cocktails in a village-like street in overlooked Woolloongabba. (p100)

Cru Bar & Cellar A long and worldly selection, with 'Holy Grail' drops by the glass. (p75)

Greenglass A showcase for small-batch Australian drops. (p32)

Cambus Wallace Dark, moody, maritime-themed bar with a Gold Coast take on cocktail classics. (p120)

Pubs

Coolangatta Hotel The hub of Coolangatta's nocturnal scene, this huge pub pumps with live bands and Sunday sessions. (p123)

Breakfast Creek Hotel A Brisbane icon with various bars and dining areas, including a beer garden, rum bar and an art-deco 'private bar' where the wooden kegs are spiked daily at noon. (p76)

Worth a Trip

Dressed in iron lacework and prettier than a wedding cake, the 1874 **Regatta Hotel** (07-3871 9595; www.regattahotel.com.au; 543 Coronation Dr, Toowong; 6.30am-1am; Regatta) is a Brisbane institution (pictured above left). Directly opposite the Regatta CityCat ferry terminal, its revamped drinking spaces include a polished, contemporary main bar, a chichi outdoor courtyard and a basement speakeasy called the Walrus Club (open 5pm to late Thursday to Saturday).

Best
LGBT

While Brisbane's LGBT scene is significantly smaller than its Sydney and Melbourne counterparts, the city has an out-and-proud queer presence. Major events on the calendar include Melt, the Queer Film Festival, and the Brisbane Pride Festival.

Bars & Clubs

Wickham Hotel This grand old dame continues to draw a chilled, mixed LGBT crowd for lazy, easy boozing. (p76)

Beat MegaClub Big with the gay and lesbian crowd, with regular drag shows and a dedicated bar, the campalicious Cockatoo Club. (p77)

Family The Sunday 'Fluffy' dance party at this megaclub is a big hit with Brisbane's younger, hotter, gay party peeps. (p74)

Festivals

Melt (www.brisbane powerhouse.org/festivals) A stimulating celebration of queer culture with 12 days of LGBT theatre, cabaret, dance, comedy, circus acts and visual arts at the Brisbane Powerhouse in January or February.

Brisbane Pride Festival (www.brisbanepride.org.au) Spread over four weeks in September, Australia's third-largest LGBT festival includes the popular Pride March and Fair Day.

Queer Film Festival (www.brisbanepowerhouse. org/festivals/brisbane-queer-film-festival) This 10-day flick fest in March showcases gay, lesbian, bisexual and transgender films from around the world, both contemporary and classic.

☑ **Top Tips**

▶ For current entertainment and events listings, interviews and articles, check out Q News (www. qnews.com.au) and Blaze (www. gaynewsnetwork. com.au).

▶ Tune in to Queer Radio (9pm to 11pm every Wednesday; www.4zzzfm.org.au), a radio show on 4ZZZ (aka FM102.1) – another source of Brisbane info. For lesbian news and views, Dykes on Mykes precedes it (7pm to 9pm Wednesday).

Best
Music

MARC GRIMWADE/GETTY IMAGES ©

Brisbane's love affair with live music began long before three lanky lads from Redcliffe sang harmonies and called themselves the Bee Gees. In more recent years successful acts, including The Veronicas, Violent Soho, DZ Deathrays and Hey Geronimo, have illustrated Brisbane's musical diversity and evolution. Cover charges for live-music acts at pubs and smaller venues start at around $5.

Live Music Venues

The Triffid Hot local and visiting bands in a WWII hangar owned by a prolific Aussie muso. (p91; pictured right)

The Zoo A Valley classic, pumping out brilliant acts playing anything from folk and indie rock, to thick and heavy hip-hop. (p77)

The Foundry Fresh, emerging Aussie talent in a purpose-built hub for bands and artists. (p70)

Brooklyn Standard Anything from funk and soul to blues and rockabilly in a speakeasy-inspired city basement. (p34)

Riverstage Evocatively set in the Botanic Gardens, this outdoor arena hosts prolific national and international music acts. (p37)

Brightside Live alternative rock plays to a worshipping crowd. (p78)

Lefty's Old Time Music Hall Atmospheric country and western in a rocking, boudoir-red honkly tonk. (p36)

Brisbane Jazz Club Straight out of the bayou, this has been Brisbane's jazz beacon since 1972. (p101)

Lock 'n' Load An upbeat crowd of music fans come to watch jazz, acoustic, roots, blues and soul acts. (p60)

Max Watt's House of Music Eclectic line-up of local and international talent plays this intimate music room. (p60)

☑ Top Tips

▶ Beyond the city's main dance clubs and party venues is an underground scene of one-off events and parties featuring some of the hottest names on the electronic music scene.

Subtrakt Events (www.subtraktevents.com)

The Kush Club (www.facebook.com/TKCBNE)

A Love Supreme (www.alovesupreme.co)

Auditree (www.facebook.com/auditree)

Wildlife Recordings (www.wildliferecordings.com)

Best
Entertainment

Most big-ticket international bands have Brisbane on their radar, and the city regularly hosts top-tier DJ talent. World-class cultural venues – among them the Queensland Performing Arts Centre and the Brisbane Powerhouse – offer a year-round program of theatre, dance, music, comedy and more. Film offerings range from mainstream to art-house, screened everywhere from multiplex cinemas to inner-city parks.

DOUG STEELEY/ALAMY STOCK PHOTO ©

Cinema

Brisbane is home to numerous cinemas, including a mainstream multiplex cinema complex at the **Myer Centre** (📞 07-3027 9999; www.eventcinemas.com.au; Level 3, Myer Centre, Elizabeth St; adult/child $18.50/13.50; ⏰ 9.45am-midnight; 🚉 Central) in central Brisbane. New Farm is home to the recently renovated New Farm Six Cinemas (p92), which offers mostly mainstream new releases. The Gallery of Modern Art (p44) runs an inspired program of international, obscure, cult and art-house film and video in its purpose-built Australian Cinémathèque.

Under the Stars

One of the best ways to spend a warm summer night in Brisbane is with a picnic basket and some friends at an outdoor cinema. Moonlight Cinema (p92) runs between December and early March at New Farm Park near the Brisbane Powerhouse. Ben & Jerry's Openair Cinemas (p60) in South Bank screen classics and recent releases at the Rainforest Green at South Bank Parklands.

☑ Top Tips

▶ You'll find entertainment news and listings at **The Music** (www.themusic.com.au), while **Q News** (www.qnews.com.au) covers the LGBT scene.

▶ **Ticketek** (www.ticketek.com.au) is a central booking agency that handles major events, sports and performances. Try **Qtix** (www.qtix.com.au) for loftier arts performances.

Performing Arts

Queensland Performing Arts Centre High-quality Australian and international theatre at Brisbane's top-tier arts venue. (p59; pictured above right)

Brisbane Powerhouse
Local and touring independent productions in a dramatic industrial setting. (p82; pictured left)

Judith Wright Centre of Contemporary Arts
Home-grown productions known for combining numerous elements, from cabaret and circus arts to dance. (p77)

Metro Arts Centre Offbeat, experimental and alternative performances in the city centre. (p37)

Arts Centre Gold Coast
A bastion of culture and civility beside the Nerang River, the Arts Centre has two cinemas, a restaurant, a bar, the Gold Coast City Gallery and a 1200-seat theatre. (p111)

Opera

Underground Opera A professional, Brisbane-based performing-arts company running annual seasons of opera and Broadway musical recitals. (p36)

Comedy

Paddo Tavern Regular, top-notch stand-up comedy spanning local, national and international names. (p38)

Brisbane Powerhouse
Numerous stand-up comedy acts throughout the year, and the hub for the annual Brisbane Comedy Festival. (p82)

Worth a Trip

Near Roma St Station in the Barracks Centre, the plush, six-screen **Palace Barracks** (07-3367 1954; www.palacecinemas.com.au; 61 Petrie Tce, Petrie Terrace; adult/concession/child $19/14.50/13; 10am-late; 375, 379), complete with bar, shows both mainstream and alternative fare. It also hosts an annual Scandinavian film festival in July and an Italian film fest in September/October. Discounted tickets are offered on Monday.

Best
Sport

Like most other Australians, Brisbanites are sports-mad. You can catch interstate and international cricket at the Gabba, south of Kangaroo Point. The cricket season runs from late September to March: if you're new to the game, try and get along to a Twenty20 match – cricket at its most explosive.

MOONBLACK/SHUTTERSTOCK ©

Spectator Sports

Gabba You can cheer both AFL football and interstate and international cricket at the Gabba in Woolloongabba, south of Kangaroo Point. (p101)

Brisbane Lions Brisbane's team in the Australian Football League (AFL). You can watch them live at a home game at the Gabba between March and September.

Brisbane Broncos NRL Rugby league is a massive spectator sport in Brizzy. The Brisbane Broncos, part of the National Rugby League (NRL; www.nrl.com.au)

competition, play home games over winter at Suncorp Stadium in Milton.

Brisbane Roar Playing at Suncorp, Brisbane Roar football (soccer) team is part of the A-League (www.aleague.com.au). The domestic football season lasts from August to February, and has been attracting fat crowds in recent years (Jade North pictured above).

Gold Coast Suns The Suns are Queensland's second AFL team, playing home matches at Metricon Stadium in Carrarra.

☑ **Top Tip**

▶ The Commonwealth Games will be held on the Gold Coast between 4 and 15 April 2018. As well as numerous venues there will be several large-screen live sites, including the Nerang Street Mall at Southport. For ticketing information and an event program, see the official site: www.gc2018.com.

Coolangatta Gold The epic Coolangatta Gold is a gruelling test of surf-lifesaving endurance.

 Best
For Free

Brisbane's parks, gardens, riverside and historic buildings can all be enjoyed free. Likewise you can leave you wallet at home and savour the beaches of the Gold Coast and the national parks and walking trails of the hinterland.

CHAMELEONSEYE/GETTY IMAGES ©

Nature

Mt Coot-tha Reserve
A huge bush reserve overlooked by 287m Mt Coot-tha and home to the botanic gardens and a planetarium. (p41)

Roma Street Parkland
One of the world's largest subtropical urban gardens. (p28)

Streets Beach
A central spot for a quick and free dip. (p46; pictured right)

Museums & Galleries

Gallery of Modern Art
The must-see GOMA focuses on Australian art from the 1970s to today. (p44)

Museum of Brisbane
An excellent, compact museum housed in City Hall. (p25)

QUT Art Museum
Regularly changing exhibits of contemporary Australian art and works by Brisbane art students. (p30)

Historic Buildings

Parliament House
The only way to get a look inside this French Renaissance–style building in the City Botanic Gardens is on one of the free tours. (p28)

Brisbane Powerhouse
A once-derelict power station that's been converted into a contemporary arts centre. (p82)

St John's Cathedral
A beautiful piece of 19th-century Gothic Revival architecture, only completed in 2009. (p29)

Old Government House
Hailed as Queensland's

☑ **Top Tip**

▶ Catch the CityHopper. Running half-hourly, this free inner-city ferry service is a gorgeous way to hop between South Bank, the CBD (Central Business District) and leafy New Farm.

most important historic building; phone for bookings. (p28)

Browsing

Davies Park Market
Organic goods and buskers aplenty. (p48)

Best
Shopping

Brisbane's retail landscape is deliciously eclectic, stretching from Vogue-indexed, high-end handbags to weekend-market arts and craft. Not surprisingly, the city's independent retailers and galleries offer the best buys, their racks, shelves and walls graced with the likes of upcycled vintage frocks, cult-label streetwear, sculptural jewellery, leather goods, bold brushstrokes and quality confectionery made with local ingredients. Cards at the ready, dive in!

Browsing Brisbane

Secondhand books, vinyl records, antique stuff and vintage fashion. Whether in boutiques, department stores or flea markets, Brisbane has a surprisingly eclectic range of goods, souvenirs and collectibles. If you're a book lover, try Archives Fine Books (p38) or Folio Books (p39) in the CBD, Scrumptious Reads (p67) in Fortitude Valley or Where the Wild Things Are (p62) in West End. Comic-book fans should definitely visit Junky Comics (p49).

Gold Coast Malls

While Brisbane has its boutiques and markets, Gold Coast has its shopping malls. Take some time from the beach and head into air-conditioned department-shopping nirvana. One of the best is sprawling **Pacific Fair** (07-5581 5100; www.pacificfair.com.au; Hooker Blvd; 9.30am-5pm Mon-Wed, Fri & Sat, to 9pm Thu, 10am-4pm Sun), a refurbed Gold Coast institution (pictured above), or just head straight to Surfers Paradise for **Circle on Cavill** (www.circleoncavill.com.au; cnr Cavill & Ferny Aves, Surfers Paradise; 9am-5.30pm Mon-Sat, 10am-4pm Sun).

CHAMELEONSEYE/SHUTTERSTOCK ©

☑ **Top Tip**

▶ Shopping 101: CBD for high-street fashion chains; Fortitude Valley for indie and cognoscenti fashion labels, local jewellery, coveted art, collectable guitar pedals and records; New Farm for antiques and retro and original artworks; South Bank and West End for gallery gift shops, market stalls, alternative books and records.

A Bit of Everything

Woolloongabba Antique Centre An epic treasure trove of vintage and retro design and fashion. (p101)

Dogstar (p39)

Fallow One of Australia's most fashion-forward men's boutiques. (p78)

Camilla Striking, colourful, resort-style threads fabulous enough for American pop royalty. (p78)

Noosa Chocolate Factory Mango-flavoured chocolate is just the prologue at this ethical Willy Wonker. (p38)

Libertine Rare, exclusive and historic fragrances made with premium natural essences. (p67)

Unique Souvenirs

Museum of Brisbane Scan the museum shop for locally made jewellery, books, wares and quirky city-themed gifts. (p25)

New Farm Confectionery High-end sweet treats made with top-quality ingredients and passion. (p88)

Young Designers Market A monthly market peddling hip, locally designed homewares, fashion and gifts. (p61)

Unique Threads

Maiocchi Playful, vintage-inspired frocks from a local designer. (p38)

Outpost Hipster workwear and out-of-the-box accessories for indie-centric guys. (p67)

Dogstar Sculptural, Japanese-influenced womenswear designed in Brisbane. (p39; pictured above)

Music

Jet Black Cat Music A much-loved West End record shop with hard-to-find vinyl, CDs and the odd, intimate in-store gig. (p49)

Butter Beats Rare, good-value discs spanning rock and reggae to trance, hip-hop, funk and more. (p79)

Record Exchange A huge collection of rare, collectable and down-right awesome LPs and CDs in the CBD. (p39)

Tym Guitars Cult-status guitar and amp store also stocking in-the-know punk, stoner and psychedelic discs. (p79)

Best
Markets

Beyond the weekly farmers markets that feed the masses in central Brisbane, New Farm and West End is a string of other fantastic local markets, peddling anything from handmade local fashion and bling, to art, skincare and out-of-the-box giftware. Half the fun is in the browsing, the chatting with stall-holders and, eventually, the buying. Hit the stalls!

JEFF GREENBERG/GETTY IMAGES ©

Farmers Markets

Jan Powers Farmers Market (p31) Central Brisbane lives out its bucolic village fantasies on Wednesday when local growers and artisans descend on Reddacliff Place to sell their prized goods. There's another one at New Farm (p83) on Saturday.

Gourmet Farmers Market The Marina Mirage mall on the Gold Coast's Main Beach fills with produce stalls every Saturday. (p111)

Davies Park Market Under a grove of huge Moreton Bay fig trees, this popular, laid-back Saturday market heaves with fresh produce, not to mention a gut-rumbling booty of multicultural food stalls. (p48; pictured above)

Weekly & Occasional Markets

Finders Keepers Markets A biannual market with more than 100 art and design stalls in a 19th-century concert hall in inner-suburban Bowen Hills. (p39)

Brisbane Riverside Markets Come Sunday, chilled-out crowds gather at the northern end of the City Botanic Gardens for this weekly food and craft market. (p31)

Collective Markets South Bank Predictably plenty of tourists, but the stalls sell some great items, including artisan leather wallets, breezy summer frocks, prints, skincare and contemporary handmade jewellery. (p63)

Young Designers Market Up to 80 of the city's best emerging designers and artists display their wares on the first Sunday of the month. (p61)

Night Markets

Eat Street Markets This is Brissie's night street-food market, with a maze of upcycled shipping containers and live bands providing the entertainment. (p109)

Boundary Street Markets Compact, twice-weekly congregation of mainly food trucks and stalls dishing up anything from Japanese noodles to crispy pancakes and vegan doughnuts on Friday and Saturday evenings. (p63)

Best
For Kids

Brisbane offers a plethora of diversions to keep young kids and teens engaged, including inner-city beach fun, bridge climbs and a string of interactive galleries and museums.

South Bank Parklands Brisbane's biggest communal playground, with barbecues, a lifeguard-patrolled beach and the slow-spinning, panoramic Wheel of Brisbane. (p46)

Brisbane River Ferry Trips The most enjoyable way to see the city is aboard a CityCat or City-Hopper ferry; the latter service is free. (p150)

Story Bridge Adventure Climb For kids 10 years and over, experience the thrill of scaling Brisbane's most famous bridge. (p97)

New Farm Park A much-loved riverside park with treehouse-inspired playground, weekend farmers market and summertime films. (p85)

Mt Coot-tha Lookout Head up to Brisbane's highest lookout for a game of spot the city landmark. (p41)

Currumbin Wildlife Sanctuary Hand-feed rainbow lorikeets. There's also kangaroo feeding, photo ops with koalas and crocodiles, reptile shows and Aboriginal dance displays. (p116; pictured above)

Currumbin Rock Pools Safe natural swimming holes 14km up Currumbin Creek Rd. (p117)

CHAMELEONSEYE/SHUTTERSTOCK ©

☑ Top Tips

▸ For current happenings check the 'Events' section of *Child* (www.childmags.com.au).

▸ Visit Brisbane (www.visitbrisbane.com.au) has a family-friendly section, with listings and itineraries.

▸ During school holidays the Brisbane City Council runs free and low-cost activities as part of its 'Chillout' program for 10- to 17-year-olds; see www.brisbane.qld.gov.au.

Best
Views

Some claim Brisbane's compact but high-rise skyline is among the prettiest of Australia's capitals, especially when illuminated buildings are reflected in the Brisbane River. The higher you go, the better the view: there are Brisbane lookouts and experiences that will open up the entire Gold Coast and hinterland.

CHAMELEONSEYE/SHUTTERSTOCK ©

Lookouts & Viewpoints

Point Danger Light
There are amazing views up and down the coast from this headland south of Coolangatta. (p123)

SkyPoint Observation Deck For an eagle-eye view of the Gold Coast and hinterland, zip up to this 230m-high observation deck (p108; pictured above)

Wheel of Brisbane
Enclosed gondolas rise to a height of nearly 60m, offering a revealing, 360-degree, inner-city panorama. (p47)

D'Aguilar National Park
If you're willing to walk there are several excellent viewpoints from this

national park, just out of the city. (p41)

Bars

Eleven The king of rooftop bars, with mesmerising views of slim-line city towers and distant Mt Coot-tha. (p73)

Mr & Mrs G Riverbar
Well-mixed cocktails, Moroccan details and killer skyscraper and water views. (p36)

Stokehouse Q The semi-alfresco bar at this high-end nosh spot serves up fantastic views and laid-back sophistication. (p56)

Sazerac Bar Brisbane's highest bar, with commanding city views for spot-the-landmark sessions. (p36)

☑ **Top Tip**

▶ For one of the best views of Brisbane and the greater metro area, head west out of the city to **Mt Coot-tha Lookout**. On a clear day you'll even spot the Moreton Bay islands and it's free! The lookout is in Mt Coot-tha Reserve, a 15-minute drive or bus ride from the city centre.

Ballooning

Balloon Down Under
Sunrise flights over the Gold Coast from Surfers Paradise, ending with a champagne breakfast. (p108)

Survival Guide

Survival Guide

Before You Go

When to Go

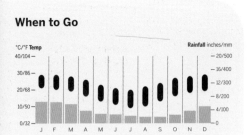

Dec–Feb Brisbane swelters during the summer months, making it the perfect time to cool off in the Gold Coast surf, dine alfresco or enjoy the many indoor air-con attractions.

May–Aug Cooler temperatures (bring a jacket) and clear blue skies make sightseeing a breeze in Brisbane, but it's still mild enough for swimming and surfing.

Sep–Nov Spring has sprung. Warmer but not too humid temperatures, perfect sightseeing weather and the hot-ticket Brisbane and Bigsound festivals.

Book Your Stay

➡ Brisbane's slumber options are varied, ranging from plush suites in heritage buildings to self-contained apartments and party-prone hostels. In general, prices do not abide by any high- or low-season rules; wavering rates usually reflect demand. Rates are often higher midweek, as well as during major events and holiday periods.

➡ Luxury names have set up in the Gold Coast in recent years, but only one resort has absolute beachfront status – the Sheraton Grand Mirage. The lack of beachfront is something of an equaliser for other options, and you can often nab a large apartment with extraordinary views and a pool one street back from the beach for a song. Backpackers are well catered for, with several hostels and a few small camping grounds.

Useful Websites

Brisbane Visitor Information & Booking Centre (www.visitbrisbane.com.au) Accommodation-booking service.

Lonely Planet (lonelyplanet.com) Recommendations and bookings.

Bed & Breakfast Site (www.babs.com.au) Unique B&Bs and guesthouses across the region.

City Hobo (www.cityhobo.com) Matches your personality with your ideal neighbourhood.

Flatmate Finders (www.flatmatefinders.com.au) Long-term share-accommodation listings.

Stayz (www.stayz.com.au) Holiday rentals.

Best Budget

Brisbane City YHA (www.yha.com.au) Smart, clean slumber pad with rooftop pool and views.

Bowen Terrace (www.bowenterrace.com.au) Tranquil, good-value lodgings in fashionable New Farm.

Bunk Backpackers (www.bunkbrisbane.com.au) A buzzing, bar-topped favourite in hedonistic Fortitude Valley.

Best Midrange

Next (www.snhotels.com/next/brisbane) A sleek, next-gen property with elegant interiors and a stylish 'In Transit' lounge for incoming and checked-out guests.

Ibis Styles (www.ibisstylesbrisbaneelizabeth.com.au) Fresh, new, upbeat digs with knockout river views in the city centre.

Tryp (www.trypbrisbane.com) Street-art themed hipness close to happening eateries, bars and clubs.

Best Top End

New Inchcolm Hotel & Suites (www.inchcolm.com.au) A Gatsby-era getaway not short on chic.

Spicers Balfour Hotel (www.spicersretreats.com/spicers-balfour-hotel) Plush, petite rooms or spacious suites in a pair of restored beauties.

Emporium (www.emporiumhotel.com.au) Polished digs, playful accents and steps away from Brisbane's best-loved see-and-be-seen strip.

Alpha Mosaic Brisbane (www.alphamosaichotelbrisbane.com.au) Slick, 18-level hotel featuring comfortable king-sized beds and contemporary decor.

Best for Families

Meriton Serviced Apartments Herschel Street (www.meritonapartments.com.au) Contemporary apartments and indoor pool in a sky-high city tower.

Mantra on Mary (www.mantra.com.au) City-centre apartments a couple of blocks from the City Botanic Gardens.

Hotel Urban Brisbane (www.hotelurban.com.au) Offers modern two-bedroom suites, plus pool and easy access to Roma Street Parklands.

Arriving in Brisbane & the Gold Coast

Brisbane Airport

Sixteen kilometres northeast of the city centre, **Brisbane Airport** (www.bne.com.au; Airport Dr) is the third-busiest airport in Australia and the main international airport serving

Brisbane and South East Queensland.

It has separate international and domestic terminals about 2km apart, linked by the **Airtrain** (📞1800 119 091; www.airtrain.com.au; adult one way/return $17.50/33), which runs every 15 to 30 minutes from 5am (6am on weekends) to 10pm (between terminals per adult/child $5/free).

It's a busy hub, with frequent domestic connections to other Australian capital cities and regional towns, as well as nonstop international flights to New Zealand, the Pacific islands, North America and Asia (with onward connections to Europe and Africa).

Gold Coast Airport

Gold Coast Airport (www. goldcoastairport.com.au; Longa Ave, Bilinga) is in Coolangatta, 25km south of Surfers Paradise. All the main Australian domestic airlines fly here. **Scoot** (www.flyscoot.com), **Air Asia** (📞1300 760 330; www. airasia.com) and **Air New Zealand** (📞13 24 76; www. airnewzealand.com.au) fly in from overseas.

Getting Around

Brisbane's excellent public-transport network – bus, train and ferry – is run by TransLink, which also runs a Transit Information Centre at Roma St Station (Brisbane Transit Centre). The tourist offices in the **city centre** (Map p26; 📞07-3006 6290; www.visitbrisbane.com.au; The Regent, 167 Queen St Mall; 🕙9am-5.30pm Mon-Thu, to 7pm Fri, to 5pm Sat, 10am-5pm Sun; 🚆Central) and **South Bank** (📞07-3156 6366; www.visitbrisbane.com. au; Stanley St Plaza, South Bank; 🕙9am-5pm; 🚆South Bank Terminal 3, 🚆South Bank) can also help with public transport information. Complementing the public-transport network is a nifty network of bike paths.

Bicycle

Brisbane has an extensive network of bikeways and shared pathways across the city and suburbs.

Brisbane's bike-share program is called **City-Cycle** (📞1300 229 253;

www.citycycle.com.au; hire per hr/day $2.20/165, 1st 30min free; 🕙24hr). To use it, you will need to subscribe via the website (per day/week $2/11), then hire a bike (additional fee) from any of the 150 stations around town. It's pricey to hire for more than an hour, so make use of the free first 30 minutes per bike and ride from station to station, swapping bikes as you go. Only a quarter of bikes include a helmet (compulsory to wear) so you may need to purchase one from shops such as Target or Kmart. You can use your Go Card to hire City Cycle bikes.

Boat

CityCat (📞13 12 30; www. translink.com.au; one way $5.60; 🕙5.25am-11.25pm) catamarans service 18 ferry terminals between the University of Queensland in St Lucia and Northshore Hamilton. Handy stops include South Bank, the three CBD terminals, New Farm Park (for Brisbane Powerhouse) and Bretts Wharf (for Eat Street Markets). Services run roughly every 15 minutes from 5.20am to around midnight. Tickets can be bought on-board or, if you have one, use your Go Card.

Free CityHopper ferries zigzag back and forth across the water between North Quay, South Bank, the CBD, Kangaroo Point and Sydney St in New Farm. These additional services start around 6am and run till about 11pm.

TransLink also runs Cross River Ferries, connecting Kangaroo Point with the CBD, and New Farm Park with Norman Park on the adjacent shore (and also Teneriffe and Bulimba further north). Ferries run every 10 to 30 minutes from around 6am to around 11pm. Fares/zones apply as per all other Brisbane transport.

For more information, including timetables, see www.brisbaneferries.com.au.

Bus

Brisbane's bus network is extensive and especially handy for reaching West End, Kangaroo Point, Woolloongabba, Fortitude Valley, Newstead and Paddington.

In the city centre, the main stops for local buses are the underground Queen Street Bus Station and King George Square Bus Station. You can also pick up many buses from the stops along Adelaide St, between George and Edward Sts.

➡ Buses generally run every 10 to 30 minutes, from around 5am (around 6am Saturday and Sunday) until about 11pm.

➡ CityGlider and BUZ services are high-frequency services along busy routes. Tickets cannot be purchased on-board CityGlider and BUZ services; use a Go Card.

➡ Free, hop-on, hop-off City Loop and Spring Hill Loop bus services circle the CBD and Spring Hill, stopping at key spots including QUT, Queen Street Mall, City Botanic Gardens, Central Station and Roma Street Parkland. Buses run every 10 minutes on weekdays between 7am and 6pm.

➡ Brisbane also runs dedicated nocturnal NightLink bus, train and fixed-rate taxi services (the latter from specified taxi ranks) from the city

and Fortitude Valley. See https://translink.com.au for details.

Car & Motorcycle

Brisbane's comprehensive public transport system will make driving unnecessary for most visitors. If you do decide to get behind the wheel, however, consider investing in a GPS; the city's convoluted streets can quickly cause frustration.

Ticketed two-hour parking is available on many streets in the CBD and the inner suburbs. Heed the signs: Brisbane's parking inspectors are pretty ruthless. During the day, parking is cheaper around South Bank and the West End than in the city centre, but it's free in the CBD in the evening from 6pm weekdays (from noon on Saturday). For more detailed information on parking, see www.visitbrisbane.com.au/parking.

Taxi

There are numerous taxi ranks in the city centre, including at Roma St Station, Treasury (corner of George and Queen Sts),

Albert St (corner of Elizabeth St) and Edward St (near Elizabeth St). You might have a tough time hailing one late at night in Fortitude Valley: there's a rank near the corner of Brunswick St and Ann St, but expect long queues. The main taxi companies are **Black & White** (☎ 13 32 22; www.blackandwhite cabs.com.au) and **Yellow Cab Co** (☎ 13 19 24; www. yellowcab.com.au).

NightLink flat-fare taxis run on Friday and Saturday nights, with dedicated ranks at Elizabeth St (corner of George St) in the city and on Warner St in Fortitude Valley.

Train

TransLink's Citytrain network has six main lines, which run as far north as Gympie on the Sunshine Coast and as far south as Varsity Lakes on the Gold Coast. All trains go through Roma St Station, Central Station and Fortitude Valley Station; there's also a handy South Bank Station.

The **Airtrain** (☎ 1800 119 091; www.airtrain.com. au; adult one way/return

$17.50/33) service integrates with the Citytrain network in the city centre and along the Gold Coast line.

Trains run from around 4.30am, with the last train on each line leaving Central Station between 11.30pm and midnight (later on Friday and Saturday). On Sunday the last trains run at around 11pm to 11.30pm.

Single train tickets can be bought at train stations, or use your **Go Card** (www.translink.com. au/tickets-and-fares/go-card; starting balance adult/child $10/5).

For timetables and a network map, see www. translink.com.au.

Essential Information

....

Business Hours

Business hours sometimes vary from season to season, but use the following as a guide:

Banks 9.30am to 4pm Monday to Friday;

some also 9am to noon Saturday

Bars 4pm to late

Cafes 7am to 5pm

Nightclubs 10pm to 4am Thursday to Saturday

Post Offices 9am to 5pm Monday to Friday; some also 9am to noon Saturday

Pubs 11am to midnight

Restaurants noon to 2.30pm and 6pm to 9pm

Shops 9am to 5pm Monday to Saturday

Supermarkets 7am to 8pm

Discount Cards

➡ The International Student Identity Card (www. isic.org), available to full-time students worldwide, yields discounts on accommodation, transport and admission to various attractions.

➡ Travellers over 60 with some form of identification (eg a Seniors Card – www.australia.gov.au/ content/seniors-card) are often eligible for concession prices at tourist attractions and on public transport.

Electricity

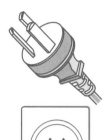

Type I
230V/50Hz

Emergency

Emergency ✆000

International Access Code ✆0011

Reverse Charges ✆1800-REVERSE (738 3773)

Money

➡ The Australian dollar comprises 100 cents. There are 5c, 10c, 20c, 50c, $1 and $2 coins, and $5, $10, $20, $50 and $100 notes.

➡ ATMs are widely available in Brisbane.

➡ Credit cards are accepted in most hotels, restaurants and cafes.

Changing Money

➡ There are foreign-exchange bureaus at Brisbane Airport's domestic and international terminals, as well as ATMs that take most international credit cards. For after-hours foreign exchange, the tellers in the Treasury Casino are there 24 hours a day.

Bargaining

➡ Bargaining and haggling aren't really part of Australian culture but there's a definite 'cash' culture where you might get a lower price on a purchase if you pay cash rather than use a credit card (thus relieving the vendor of some of their official tax obligations).

Public Holidays

New Year's Day
1 January

Australia Day
26 January

Easter (Good Friday to Easter Monday inclusive) March or April

Anzac Day 25 April

Labour Day First Monday in May

Queen's Birthday
Second Monday in June

Royal Queensland Show Day (Brisbane only) Second or third Wednesday in August

Christmas Day
25 December

Boxing Day
26 December

Safe Travel

➡ Brisbane is a relatively safe place to visit, but take reasonable precautions.

➡ Don't leave hotel rooms or cars unlocked or valuables visible through car windows.

➡ As in all major cities, avoid poorly lit areas and parks after dark.

➡ Floods and violent storms are a fact of life in Brisbane, especially during the rainier summer months. Pay attention to warnings from local authorities.

Toilets

➡ Toilets in Brisbane are sit-down Western style.

➡ Public toilets are usually free and commonly found in shopping centres, department stores, cultural centres and parks, as well as bars, cafes and restaurants.

Tourist Information

Brisbane Visitor Information & Booking Centre (Map p26; ✆07-3006 6290; www.visitbrisbane.com. au; The Regent, 167 Queen St Mall; ⏱9am-5.30pm Mon-Thu, to 7pm Fri, to 5pm Sat, 10am-5pm Sun; 🚆Central) is Brisbane's main tourist information centre, providing maps, information about attractions and events, as well as offering accommodation-booking services.

You'll find another visitor information centre across the river in **South Bank** (✆07-3156 6366; www.visitbrisbane.com.au; Stanley St Plaza, South Bank; ⏱9am-5pm; 🚋South Bank Terminal 3, 🚆South Bank).

Travellers with Disabilities

➡ Brisbane's city centre is commendably wheelchair-friendly and Brisbane City Council (BCC) produces the *Brisbane Mobility Map*. It's usually available from the **BCC Customer Services Centre** (✆07-3407 2861; www.brisbane.qld.gov.au; 266 George St; ⏱9am-5pm Mon-Fri; 🚋North Quay, 🚆Central), as well as online.

➡ The Queensland State Government's **Disability Awareness Information Line** (✆07-3224 8444, toll-free 1800 177 120) provides information on disability services and support throughout Queensland. Its phone lines are open from 9am to 5pm Monday to Friday.

➡ For information about disabled access on public transport, see www.translink.com.au/travel-with -us/accessibility.

➡ Download Lonely Planet's free Accessible Travel guide from http://lptravel. to/AccessibleTravel.

Visas

➡ All visitors to Australia need a visa – only New Zealand nationals are exempt, and even they sheepishly receive a 'special category' visa on arrival.

➡ There are several different visas available, depending on your nationality and what kind of visit you're contemplating.

➡ See the website of the **Department of Immigration & Border Protection** (✆1300 363 263, 02-6275 6666; www.border.gov.au) for info and application forms (also available from Australian diplomatic missions overseas and travel agents), plus details on visa extensions, Working Holiday Visas (417) and Work and Holiday Visas (462).

Behind the Scenes

Send Us Your Feedback

We love to hear from travellers – your comments help make our books better. We read every word, and we guarantee that your feedback goes straight to the authors. Visit **lonelyplanet.com/contact** to submit your updates and suggestions.

Note: We may edit, reproduce and incorporate your comments in Lonely Planet products such as guidebooks, websites and digital products, so let us know if you don't want your comments reproduced or your name acknowledged. For a copy of our privacy policy visit lonelyplanet.com/privacy.

Acknowledgements

Cover photograph: Surfers Paradise beach, Andrew Watson/AWL ©
Contents photograph: Brisbane's waterfront cityscape, Andrey Orekhov/500px ©

Cristian's Thanks

First and foremost, an epic thank you to Drew Westbrook for his hospitality and generosity. Sincere thanks also to Craig Bradbery, Tim Crabtree, Amy Ratcliffe, Leanne Layfield, Terese Finegan, Michael Flocke, Simon Betteridge, Annabel Sullivan, Garry Judd and the many locals who offered insight and insider knowledge along the way. At Lonely Planet, a huge thanks to Tasmin Waby for her support and encouragement.

Donna's Thanks

Love and gratitude to Juliette Claire for her inspiration and incredible regional knowledge. Thanks to ex-locals Peter Maclaine and Debbie Wheeler, especially for Pete's surfing expertise. Thanks to Harry in Broadbeach, to the Byron skydivers and to Amanda and Simon in Brunswick Heads for great hospo insights. Thanks also to Nic Wrathall for your company during some long research days, and Brigid Healy and Andrew King, Kate Dale and Darryn Devlin for Sydney homecoming love. Finally thanks to Joe Guario, for everything.

This Book

This 1st edition of Lonely Planet's *Pocket Brisbane & the Gold Coast* guidebook was researched and written by Paul Harding, Cristian Bonetto and Donna Wheeler. This guidebook was produced by the following:

Destination Editor Tasmin Waby **Product Editors** Grace Dobell, Carolyn Boicos **Senior Cartographer** Julie Sheridan **Book Designer** Nicholas Colicchia **Assisting Editors** Gabrielle Innes, Helen Koehne, Susan Paterson, Gabrielle Stefanos

Cartographer Rachel Imeson **Cover Researcher** Campbell McKenzie **Thanks to** Jennifer Carey, Heather Champion, Daniel Corbett, Megan Eaves, MaSovaida Morgan, Catherine Naghten, Martine Power, Kirsten Rawlings, Clifton Wilkinson, Amanda Williamson

Index

See also separate subindexes for:

⊗ **Eating p158**

⊕ **Drinking p159**

✪ **Entertainment p159**

🔒 **Shopping p159**

Our Writers

Paul Harding

As a writer and photographer, Paul has been travelling the globe for the best part of two decades, with an interest in remote and offbeat places and cultures. He's an author and contributor to more than 50 Lonely Planet guides to countries and regions as diverse as India, Iceland, Belize, Vanuatu, Iran, Indonesia, New Zealand, Finland and – his home patch – Australia.

Cristian Bonetto

Cristian has contributed to over 30 Lonely Planet guides to date, including *New York City, Italy, Venice & the Veneto, Naples & the Amalfi Coast, Denmark, Copenhagen, Sweden* and *Singapore*. When not on the road, you'll find the reformed playwright and TV scriptwriter slurping espresso in his beloved hometown, Melbourne.

Donna Wheeler

Donna has written guidebooks for Lonely Planet for 10 years, including the *Italy, Norway, Belgium, Africa, Tunisia, Algeria, France, Austria* and *Melbourne* titles. She became a travel writer after various careers as a commissioning editor, creative director, digital producer and content strategist.

Published by Lonely Planet Global Limited
CRN 554153
1st edition – Nov 2017
ISBN 978 1 78657 700 9
© Lonely Planet 2017   Photographs © as indicated 2017
10 9 8 7 6 5 4 3 2 1
Printed in Malaysia